Forgotten Reformer

Myles Coverdale

Errata – p198

How shall they **preach** except they be sent?

Copyright © 2021 by G F Main

All rights reserved. No part of this book may be reproduced or used in any manner without written permission of the copyright owner except for the use of quotations in a book review. For more information, please email: gandsmain@gmail.com

First Published: June 2021

ISBN Number: 978-1-9168737-0-4

Cover picture: Exeter Cathedral

Forgotten Reformer: Myles Coverdale

and the first 40 years of the English Reformation

Woodcut from Coverdale's 1535 Bible: The grapes of Eshcol

G F Main

Contents

1	Introduction	1
2	England before the Reformation	6
3	The dawn of the Reformation	20
4	First exile. The 1535 Coverdale Bible	45
5	Working for Thomas Cromwell	62
6	Second exile. Suffering reproach	84
7	Reformation gathers pace. The days of Edward VI	110
8	Bishop of Exeter	127
9	A narrow escape from burning	141
10	Third exile. A wanderer	152
11	Last years. An early Puritan	170
12	An evaluation	195

Appendix One: Comparison of Bible versions	206
Appendix Two: The Martyrdom of Joan Waste, an answer of Anne Askew	208
Appendix Three: Coverdale's most important literary works	210
Appendix Four: Letter written by Coverdale in anticipation of being burned at the stake	214
End notes	218

Acknowledgments

My sincere thanks are due to the following:

Professor Alec Ryrie of Durham University, for helpful suggestions at an early stage.

Neil Adams of the Borthwick Institute for Archives, University of York; John Armstrong, Assistant Archivist, St Peter's School, York; for generously giving of their time to hunt for clues as to Coverdale's early life. Sarah Griffin, York Minster Librarian; for introducing me to the world of lost books as I searched in vain for the 1569 biography of Coverdale. James Richards, Rector of St Martin's Windermere for tracing the inscription in his church to the Bishop's Bible, which saved me from a mistake made by other writers. Rebecca Browning provided me with pictures of Sudeley Castle, as did the Bergzabern Tourist office of their town.

Research of Coverdale's life at Cambridge has involved the following who have been very helpful: Colin Higgins, Librarian at St Catharine's College; Lizzie Ennion-Smith, Archivist Pembroke College; John Wagstaff, Librarian at Christ's College; and Dr Katherine Krick for helpful suggestions concerning the Austin Friary, Cambridge; Mark Statham for tracing for me the 1535 Almanac at Gonville and Caius College Library.

Ellie Jones, Exeter Cathedral Archivist; and Scott Pettit, Senior Archivist at Devon Archives and Local Studies Service contributed in providing documents from Coverdale's time as Bishop of Exeter. In particular, I wish to thank Scott for sending to me the two volumes of Coverdale's Episcopal registers.

Emily Naish, Archivist at Salisbury Cathedral; gave useful information re Sir John Macalpine. Sarah Radcliffe, Archivist at St Paul's Cathedral helped with the Coverdale concordance.

Dr George Ella's familiarity with resources in German-speaking areas across four countries and 50 archives has been of value. Jacques Erard of the University of Geneva sent photos of the Reformation Wall.

Mr Steve Taylor of the Evangelical Library made available Lupton's work on the Geneva Bible. Mrs Julia Button provided material from the archives of her late father, Mr Lewis Lupton.

Dr Helen Carron gave access to Emmanuel College Cambridge archive material on Coverdale. Hannah Dunmow provided the file on Coverdale held in the archives of the Clothworkers' Company

Hugh Cahill, Senior Librarian, Lambeth Palace Library; helped in tracing Church of England records re Myles Coverdale, and also gave access to the Richard Bertie papers. The staff at the Bodleian Library Oxford and the British Library were both helpful and professional.

Dr Douglas Somerset and Mr J E North gave critical scrutiny to the mss. Stephen Pickles ran his expert eye over this work and made many helpful suggestions and corrections. Dr Matthew Hyde and Jeremy Walker gave helpful hints on publishing, and Timothy Wiltshire turned the finished document into something the printers could work with. My wife, Sheila, has been invaluable for both editorial and proof-reading input and Mrs Myra Muriana has kindly standardised my erratic style with her meticulous checking and proof-reading. Finally, Mrs Rachel Alderman and Miss Marion Hyde checked through the finished mss for interest and readability.

Vocabulary

Lutheran – is used throughout to denote a) the German and Danish churches which followed the teaching of Martin Luther. b) The distinctive teaching of Luther on the Lord's Supper. The Anglican Church is described as Lutheran up to the death of Henry VIII because of the large influence of Luther's writings in England, as in other countries in the early years of the Reformation.

Reformed – denotes those, other than Lutherans, who embraced the Reformation. In particular, the influence of John Calvin began to be felt throughout Western Europe by 1540. The Anglican Church from the beginning of the reign of Edward VI had adopted Calvinist articles of faith but not for the most part their practices in worship.

Protestant – the term relates to the protest by the German princes in 1529. The narrative in this work does not use the term except in relation to the political issues during the reigns of Edward VI and Elizabeth I. This is for two reasons: a) the narrative begins well before 1529 b) in the early days the term Protestant described the German struggle for freedom of worship against the opposition of Emperor Charles V, to which only glancing reference is made in this account.

All mistakes are my own, as are many of the pictures. Any reader spotting a factual error is welcome to contact the author at gandsmain@gmail.com

The quotations at the head of each chapter are from Coverdale's 1535 Bible.

The National Archives calculator states that £1 in the money of 1540 is worth £420 today.

Finally, whosoever thou be, take these words of Scripture into thy heart, and be not an outward hearer but a doer, and practise thyself therein; that thou mayest feel in thine heart the sweet promises thereof for thy consolation in all trouble, and for the sure stablishing of thy hope in Christ; ... that the Holy Scripture may have free passage, and be had in reputation, to the worship of the author thereof, which is even God himself; to whom for His blessed word be glory and dominion now and ever, Amen.

(Coverdale's Prologue to the first printed Bible in English 1535)

Europe in 1540

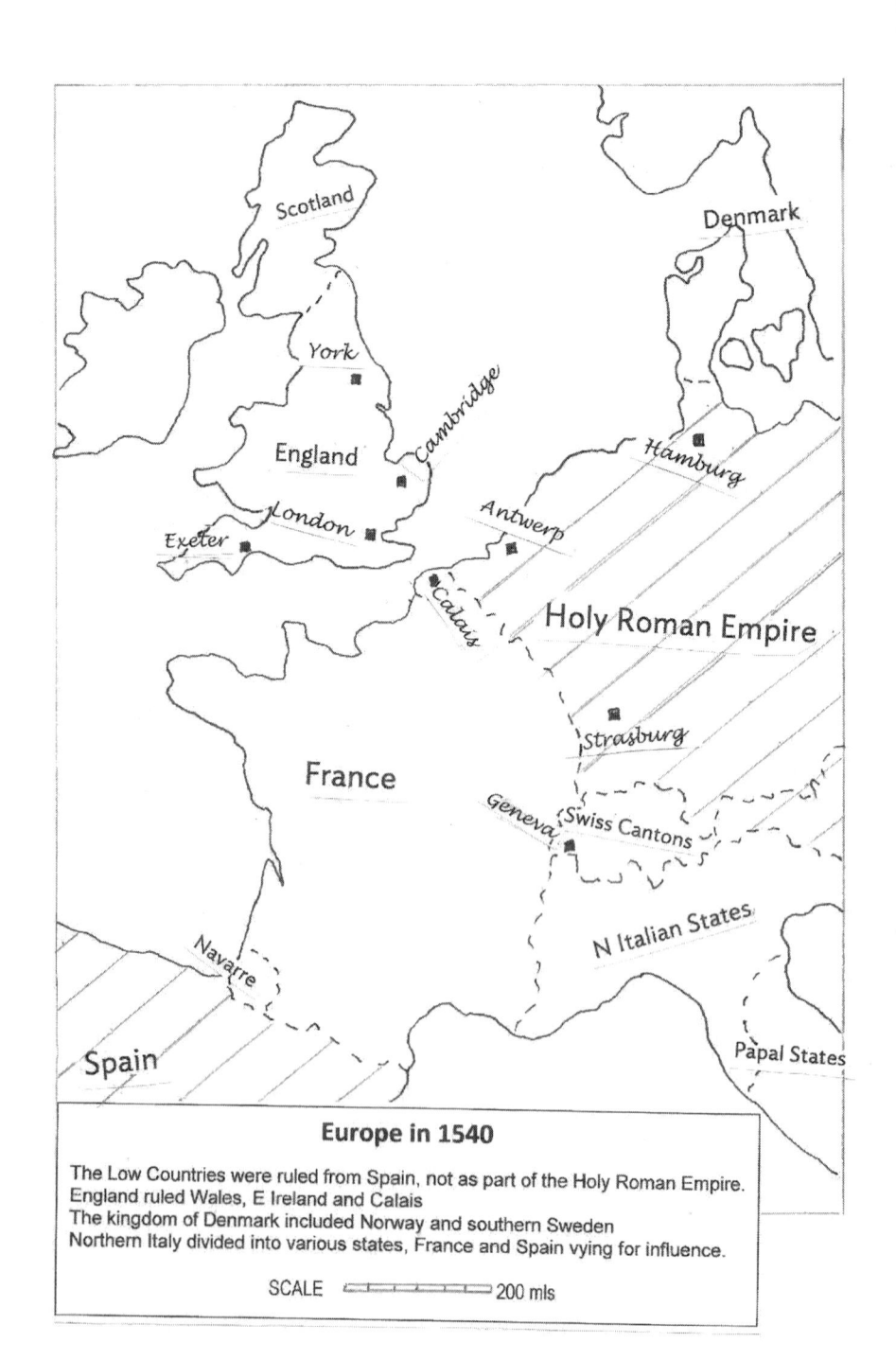

The Low Countries were ruled from Spain, not as part of the Holy Roman Empire.
England ruled Wales, E Ireland and Calais
The kingdom of Denmark included Norway and southern Sweden
Northern Italy divided into various states, France and Spain vying for influence.

SCALE 200 mls

Chapter 1

Introduction

And I thank Christ Jesus our Lord, which hath made me strong, for he counted me faithful, and put me in office, when before I was a blasphemer, a persecutor, a tyrant: but I obtained mercy, because I did it ignorantly in unbelief. Nevertheless the grace of our Lord was more abundant through faith and love which is in Christ Jesus. (I Timothy 1 block C)

In the summer of 1527, the monastery doors of the Austin Friary in Cambridge shut for the last time on Myles Coverdale as he left the life of a Roman Catholic monk and priest for that of a reformer and preacher. He was thirty-eight years old. For some thirteen years he had been a priest, trying to earn salvation by his good works and by a careful, exact observance of religious duties. These would have included saying mass, hearing confession, doing penance and creeping to a wooden cross. From this time forward his life was changed. The above quotation from his 1535 English Bible describes exactly that change. It was to be a life of poverty, exile, hardship and danger, but one he chose willingly. This is the story of his life.

Why write a life of Myles Coverdale? First, although we know little of his first thirty-eight years, the remainder of his life is brim-full of interest, spanning the first forty years of the

Reformation in England. He was a very significant figure in that Reformation.

- Coverdale was one of a group of scholars at Cambridge in the early 1520s, where the light of the Reformation dawned in England. Most of this group were burned at the stake for their beliefs, from Thomas Bilney in 1531 to Hugh Latimer in 1556.
- Very soon after becoming a preacher, he fled into exile to help William Tyndale with the dangerous work of translating the Bible into English. This work cost Tyndale his life. By the time of Tyndale's death after sixteen months in prison, Coverdale had completed the first printed English Bible.
- Returning to England after Henry VIII had transferred the headship of the Church of England from the Pope to himself, Coverdale was active in a variety of ways in support of the King's chief minister, Thomas Cromwell.
- As Henry VIII turned against the Reformation, beginning with the execution of Thomas Cromwell in 1540, Coverdale went into a second exile. He spent the next eight years in Lutheran Germany, preaching, teaching and translating works of Luther and others into English.
- On his return when Edward VI was enthroned, Coverdale was appointed chaplain to Katherine Parr (sixth and surviving wife of Henry VIII) and after her death became Bishop of Exeter. This was the time of the rebellion in the West Country over the issue of the Prayer Book, and he was in much personal danger, being one of very few Reformation preachers in Devon and Cornwall.
- At the start of Queen Mary's reign, Coverdale was deprived and summoned to London, this time fully expecting to be burnt at the stake with the other

leading ministers of the Reformation: Cranmer, Ridley, Latimer, Hooper, Rogers and Bradford.
- Remarkably, his life was saved by the intervention of Christian III, King of Denmark. Coverdale was the only one of the prisoners who was voluntarily released by the Queen without denying his faith, and he went a third time into exile, ending in Geneva where he joined John Knox's church. Like Knox, he was greatly influenced by the order and simplicity of the Genevan churches.
- From here, in 1559, he returned to spend the last ten years of his life in London; uneasy with the Elizabethan Church of England settlement and increasingly unwilling to conform.

Portrait of Coverdale

A second reason for studying his life, is that there are references to Coverdale in biographies of almost all the leading figures of the Reformation, including Knox, Cranmer, Cromwell, Latimer, Tyndale and Edward VI, whose lives he touched, and about whom much has been written. There have been, for example, seven major biographies of Thomas Cromwell since the year 2000. However, little has been written about Coverdale, justifying a label of *The Forgotten Reformer*. The best known book is by J F Mozley (1953), who wrote one chapter on Coverdale's life and fourteen on his translation work. Two other biographies exist: one by J J Lowndes written in 1838, the other by gifted artist Lewis Lupton, is found in volumes 11 and 12 of *The History of the Geneva Bible* published in the 1970s. Unsurprisingly, the eminent historian A G Dickens described Coverdale as *a major and too often neglected figure of the English Reformation.* [1]

The third reason for writing is that the Reformation brought the English-speaking world out of the Middle Ages, laying the foundation of many benefits we enjoy to this day. It was first and foremost a spiritual and religious work. However, one fears that much of this heritage is buried in the land of forgetfulness. In forty years of teaching, for example, I have found that most History students to whom I have spoken who have studied the topic, tend to think the Reformation in England was Henry VIII's divorce, with the resulting political and social changes. Otherwise it is mistaken for the Renaissance of learning with which Erasmus is closely connected. This book is a small attempt to redress the balance.

However, two formidable difficulties lie in the way of writing about Coverdale. The first is that only seven snippets of information are known about the first thirty-eight years of his life to 1527. While we have details of the conversion of his fellow students and friars, Latimer and Bilney, we know nothing of what caused the change in Coverdale, bringing him from a religion of works to one of faith.

Secondly, he spent some 20 years of the remaining years of his life in three exiles. The times were very dangerous. Much of Europe was ruled by Charles V of Spain, Germany and the Holy Roman Empire. The next most powerful figure was Francis I of France. Both rulers competed for the support of the Pope in their Italian wars and were avowed enemies of this tiny band of reformers. When events in England caused the reformers to flee, the best refuge was to remain in hiding, often under assumed names. During his second exile, Coverdale used the pen name Michael Angelus

An important aspect of the lives of the early leaders of the Reformation was their single-mindedness. Once Coverdale and others came to believe that the will of God is found in the Bible and its teaching, rather than through the authority of the Church, they were willing to endure hardship, poverty, exile and persecution rather than accept the laws of king and church, when they came into conflict with their convictions. Hear Coverdale's own words:

In this world must we seek no high honour nor praise, but willingly humble and submit ourselves under the rebuke and cross with Christ our Head. Christ also exhorteth us to follow His footsteps and do after His example, and not to forsake the truth and love of our neighbour for their hatred; but constantly to do our best to guide all men unto God. And if for such our faithfulness and love there happen reproach and trouble to us, we ought to rejoice, that God doth us so great honour, as to suffer somewhat for His name's sake. [2]

Chapter 2

England before the Reformation

And therefore get thee up by times, for the light cometh, and the glory of the Lord shall rise up upon you. For lo, while the darkness and clouds covereth the earth and the people, the Lord shall show the light and his glory shall be seen in thee. The gentiles shall come to thy light, and kings to the brightness that springeth forth upon thee. (Isaiah 60 block A)

England as it was in the first thirty-eight years of Coverdale's life is obscure to us and little understood. To appreciate the struggles of the Reformers to achieve change, a short description of the society and religion of that era is needful.

State of English society

England and Scotland were independent countries, with much lawlessness and banditry on the borders between the two nations. Nicholas Ridley tells us: *Where I was born, not far from the Scottish borders, I have known my countrymen watch night and day in their harness, and their spears in their hands, especially if they had any warning of the coming of the Scots. And so doing, at every bickering some of them lost their lives.* [1] War between the two nations was a recurring event in the Middle Ages, sometimes with devastating consequences. The battle of Flodden, fought in 1513 between the two nations when Coverdale was a young man, saw a great slaughter:

casualties included the Scottish King James IV and the flower of his nobility, leaving his infant son as king.

The English kings ruled over England, Wales, Ireland plus a small area around Calais, on the French side of the Channel. With no royal standing army, the power of the nobility was great, especially at a distance from London. So the extent to which royal Tudor policy was carried out often depended on the local nobles. When, for example, the Prayer Book rebellion in Devon was to be put down in 1549, Lord John Russell, the 1st Earl of Bedford, was sent by the Privy Council to deal with it, he being the biggest landowner in Devon. Coverdale went with him as chaplain to the army.

England was a rural country of poor roads and little trade; most of the population engaged in a hand-to-mouth existence. Bread was the staple of life, providing some 80% of a peasant's nutrition, and life was short. Healthy adults were old by the time they reached the age of 55. [2] Coverdale was exceptional in living to 81 years of age. Death was ever present, with up to one third of children not reaching adulthood. Childbirth itself was often hazardous and dangerous to the mothers. However, if spared through their years of childbearing, women usually outlived their husbands. There were many aged widows in the land.

Every winter the dark cold days, shortage of food, poor sanitation and lack of work would raise the death rate among the three to four million people who lived in Great Britain and Ireland. In addition, from time to time the plague would sweep through the land, carrying away old and young, strong and frail. Myles Coverdale himself caught the plague in his old age in London in 1563 but remarkably he recovered and lived a further six years. That outbreak is described by his friend John Foxe:

For two years the plague raged in London – from the first of January 1562, to the last of December 1563. There died in the city 17,404 persons from this disease, besides above 3000 from other causes. Forasmuch remarks John Stowe, who wrote from personal recollection, as the poor citizens were this year plagued with a threefold plague, pestilence, scarcity of money and dearth of victuals – the misery whereof were too long here to write; no doubt the poor remember it, the rich by flight into the counties made shift for themselves. [3]

One of the few facts we know of the early life of Myles Coverdale is that he was born in York. Records of any sort from 1488 are very sparse, but during his third exile we understand from Mozley's research that: *In a list of exiles who settled at Aarau in 1557, he is described as Miles Coverdale, born in a town (dorf) named York, formerly Bishop of Exeter.* Now this list is careful in its description of places: *where it means county it says Herrschaft; where it means town it says dorf.* [4] Before this discovery, most writers assumed Coverdale was born in the Coverdale area of North Yorkshire, near Richmond.

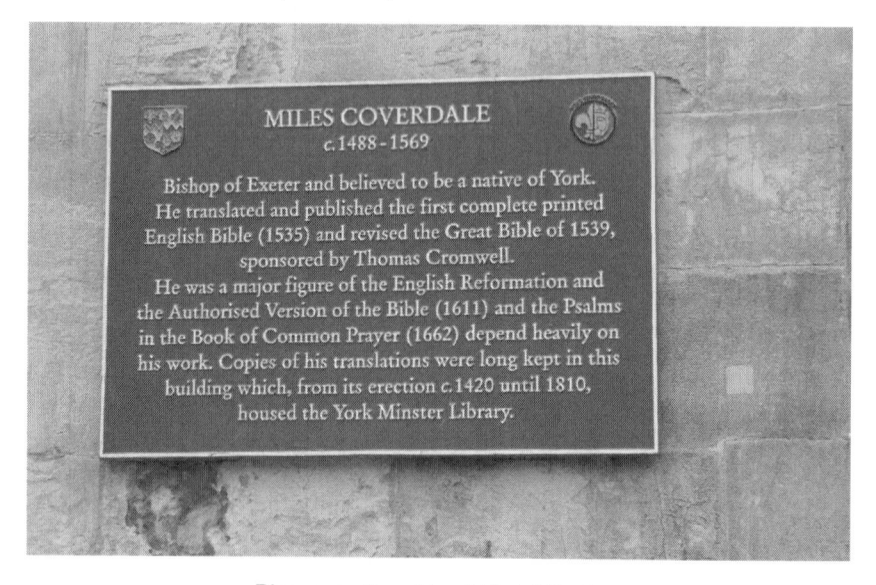

> **MILES COVERDALE**
> c.1488-1569
>
> Bishop of Exeter and believed to be a native of York. He translated and published the first complete printed English Bible (1535) and revised the Great Bible of 1539, sponsored by Thomas Cromwell.
> He was a major figure of the English Reformation and the Authorised Version of the Bible (1611) and the Psalms in the Book of Common Prayer (1662) depend heavily on his work. Copies of his translations were long kept in this building which, from its erection c.1420 until 1810, housed the York Minster Library.

Plaque on the side of York Minster

There were few towns in England in that era. London was by far the biggest with a population of about 50,000. [5] It was of great importance in England as the residence of the kings and centre of government. The five Tudor monarchs mostly lived in their palaces just beyond its gates. Wealth in its greatest concentration was found here too, with a sizeable merchant class in the City, trading from the port of London. England's biggest export was wool. Other towns were few and far between.

York was the largest of the towns in northern England with some 5,000 people. It was the northern centre of both the Church and the wool trade. The river Ouse was navigable as far as the city, and the town had its own Merchant Adventurers' Hall, a busy market place where merchants from far and near could trade. However, northern England was remote and impoverished compared with the South. This can be illustrated by the levy demanded by Henry VIII of the Church of England in 1531. The diocese of Canterbury, covering southern England, was judged capable of paying £100,000, and York, which administered the northern half of the country £19,000.

Cardinal Wolsey was Archbishop of York for 16 years. Neither Coverdale, nor any other resident would ever have seen him there, however, being an absentee in London until he was sent to York in disgrace a few months before his death in 1529. Being the seat of one of the two English archbishops, York also attracted several friaries and monasteries. These had their own liberties and often, if a man was wanted for misdeeds in the town, he could escape into one of the monasteries which had their own laws and courts. They represented a significant part of the population.

Nothing is known of Myles Coverdale's early education. We have testimony of Bishop Bale who knew Coverdale well in later years that *he was an excellent learner, who drank in learning with a burning thirst* and of John Hooker that *from his childhood (he was) given to learning, wherein he profited much.* [6] York had two excellent schools, and some of the monastic centres would also in those days have had Almoners' schools to teach the children of the poor. Coverdale may well have had access to what learning was available, including knowledge of the Latin tongue and to what few English and Latin books were available. Printed books were almost unknown in his childhood as William Caxton's London printing press, the first in England, only began work in 1476.

The Church at the start of the Reformation

There were some 30,000 priests in England in 1500, when Coverdale was getting his education. He joined their ranks in 1514, being ordained by the Bishop of Norwich. The order of priest required the candidate to be 24 years of age, and gave the right to 'offer the Host', lead prayers and preach. In theory they were men of sound learning, able to read and speak Latin, but in practice only 10% went through one of the five universities in Great Britain (two in England, three in Scotland). In Ireland there were no universities. To become a parish priest, one simply had to be nominated by a patron, often one of the gentry, sometimes the king, or a bishop. There were many absentee clergy, or sometimes one holding several benefices which would increase his income, but not his work unless he chose to do more. The practice of simony, bribing one's way into office, was illegal but widespread in 1500.

The Roman Catholic Church and its priests were a key influence in England at this time. The Church in England was divided into 9,000 parishes, each with its church building, and a priest responsible for the spiritual welfare of his parishioners. The chief source of income for the parish was tithing – the giving of one tenth of the value of each man's labour to the Church. One third was to provide for the priests, one third for the upkeep of the buildings, and one third for the relief of the poor. While, understandably, many of the poor did their best to keep payments to a minimum, they were powerless to withhold payments when demanded. The Church also owned large tracts of land, as did many monasteries. [7]

Pre-Reformation Church at Brinklow, Warwickshire. The stone images on the four corners of the tower were removed at the Reformation.

The churches were colourful places pre-Reformation, often with large detailed paintings of the Last Judgment and a number of stone and wooden images. The most important image was the 'rood loft'. This was a life-sized wooden image of Christ on the cross, with the Virgin Mary on one side and the apostle John on the other. The heart of the church was the altar rather than the pulpit; preaching was rare, and very few churches had pews. Rather the congregation would move about, standing in front of a stone image while saying their prayers, or talking and conducting business. Participation in the service was very limited, with typically only the choir chanting or singing. Timperley tells us that as far as congregations were concerned: *such music was three times removed from the people: by the foreign language, by elaboration which disguised the text and by their own non-participation.* [8]

Levels of education among the clergy were not high. Wilson tells us that of the 869 wills of clergy proved at Norwich, between 1500 and 1550, only 158 died possessing books at all, and only twelve testators owned Latin Bibles. *The vast majority were concerned only with the mechanical performance of their pastoral, ritual and sacramental duties.*[9]

The services were read in Latin, but often the lesser clergy did not understand that language. The clergy were mostly there to pray for their flock and to celebrate the sacraments on their behalf. To do this they wore vestments, coloured robes in harmony with the altar cloths. The priests were a class above the ordinary lay person, distinct and separate from them. *It was a medieval truism that one Paternoster (the Lord's Prayer) said at a priest's behest had the same weight as 100,000 said by a lay person's own initiative – just one sign of the authority which was attached to the priesthood.* [10]

The priest vowed to remain unmarried for life: by the year 1500 celibacy had for four centuries been a requirement of Church life. When Myles Coverdale joined the ranks of the priesthood in 1514, his vow would have bound him to a single life. Like many of the Reformers, however, he married after leaving the Austin Friary in Cambridge and embraced family life. Coverdale was fifty years of age when he married Elizabeth Macheson. When he was Bishop of Exeter, one of the merchants of the city, John Hooker, gave her this testimony: *His wife a most sober, chaste and godly matron: his house and household another church, in which was exercised all godliness and virtue.* [11] They were married for about 26 years, she sharing the hardship and poverty of his second and third exiles, dying in London in 1565, four years before he did. He remarried the following year, his second wife Katherine caring for him to the end of his life.

The Austin Friary

Our first real glimpse of Coverdale was as a member of the Austin Friary at Cambridge. No record has been discovered of Coverdale's enrolment at any of the colleges, suggesting that, while studying in the university he was in the Austin Friary, perhaps transferring from that of York. The Austin Friars were founded in 1256 by Pope Alexander IV, being an amalgam of five groups of hermits. They were to wear black robes, a hood and a leather belt. It is estimated that there were in England 550 Austin friars in 1450, dwindling to 300 at the time of the closure of their houses by Thomas Cromwell in 1538. [12] The most important houses were in London, with several in East Anglia as well as Cambridge and York. Novices were received at the age of fourteen, and would later spend three years at one of the universities if they wished to engage in higher studies. Although the various monasteries in Cambridge were built to house members of their orders, they were used for academic purposes too, functioning like the colleges and forming an integral part of the University

The Austin Friars maintained a strict and careful round of religious duties within the Friary, as well as one of good works outside. They were not allowed personal property, but had all things common. *The Divine Office was a central and recurrent feature of the daily life of the Austin Friars; it began with Matins at midnight, and the friars chanted Lauds at dawn when they awoke, after which there was the conventual Mass, to which everyone was obliged to attend. After lunch was Vespers and the evening meal was followed by Compline.* [13]

However the friars, being but human, could not always live to the standards of perfection set. The regime of the Austin Friars included the use of fastings, flagellations (beatings) and a monastic prison for those guilty of 'transgressions'. At the important London Friary, there were reports from the prior Edmund Bellond at this time of drunkenness, immoral behaviour, disrupting mass and wasting money. [14]

In 1516, Pope Leo X licensed the Austin Friars to sell indulgences. The money was to be shared between the curia (central Church office) and the Friars. The receipts kept by Bellond, recorded for the five years that the indulgences were offered, that is 1517 to 1521, the astonishing revenue of £1114 14s 9.5d (worth over £500,000 today), which was just the fifty percent taken by the friars. [15] It was a similar sale of indulgences at the same time in Germany that provoked another Austin Friar, Martin Luther, to nail his ninety-five theses to the church door at Wittenberg.

The centrality of the Mass in pre-Reformation England

Writing from prison at the start of Queen Mary's reign thirty years later, and fully expecting to lay down his life with the other leading Reformers, Coverdale had this to say: *How horrible things are contained in the mass book I learned many years ago, which I utterly abhor* (see Appendix 4). This one central issue of the way sins can be forgiven did more to separate Reformers from the Church of Rome than any other. Time and again, had they been willing to concede transubstantiation, their lives would have been spared in the reign of both Henry VIII and Mary.

What was the teaching of the Church? The most important church service was the Mass – said in Latin. The service involved two key beliefs. The first was transubstantiation. This was the belief that when the priest celebrates Mass, the bread (wafer) and wine are physically transformed into the glorified but fully human body of Christ. This became official Roman Catholic teaching at the Lateran Council of 1215: *The sacrifice is identical with the sacrifice of Christ on the cross, inasmuch as Jesus Christ is a priest and victim both. The only difference lies in the manner of the offering... bloodless on our altars.* [16]

The second belief of the Church was that when the penitent had the wafer placed in his mouth by the priest, then he received the complete body and blood of Christ, together with his soul and divinity and so received the forgiveness of sins. The host (a consecrated wafer) was lifted by the priest above his head in adoration. Communicants would then advance to the altar and kneel, whereupon the priest would place a piece of bread in their open mouth. Only the priest could touch the bread, otherwise it became polluted. Only the priest would partake of the wine.

Because the Mass was designed to re-enact the experience of Christ, from the upper room through the judgment hall to his death and resurrection, the ceremony was an extended and complicated liturgy, performed with great artistry by the priest. He must make the sign of the cross, kiss the altar, fold his hands, strike his breast, and pray aloud a number of times in sequence. His highly coloured robes, candles, bells, incense and music were all designed to enhance the drama of the occasion

The Mass was considered to be of great importance to the dead as well as the living. Their consciences told men that they had committed sin and were therefore not fit for heaven. Consequently, they expected to find themselves in purgatory (a place of temporary punishment) after death – to suffer for a time to atone for sins committed in life. The Mass then, which had to be paid for, became the means of extracting the souls of the dead from purgatory. When he died in 1509 Henry VII, the first Tudor king, left money sufficient for 10,000 Masses to be said for his soul and those of others. The Mass was thus a considerable generator of income to the pre-Reformation Church.

The Church hierarchy

Hampton Court Palace, built by Cardinal Wolsey for his London home.

The most powerful man in England in 1520 was Thomas Wolsey, Archbishop of York, Papal Legate, Lord Chancellor and Cardinal; a man of energy, vanity and great ambition. His progress in public was marked by a train of knights, priests, retainers and officials, preceded by two silver crosses – proclaiming his temporal and spiritual power. Under the king he was all-powerful. Three times had he come close to becoming Pope, and the monuments to his pride, wealth and power: Hampton Court Palace and Cardinal (now Christ Church) College, Oxford endure to this day. One part of his authority, and that of other bishops, was through the Church courts. These settled minor civil disputes between parishioners and could levy fines. Their most serious role though, was in trying for heresy those who did not conform to the teachings of the Church.

In 1401, shortly after the death of John Wycliffe and over 80 years before the birth of Coverdale, the bishops persuaded Parliament to bring in heresy laws. The most serious punishment for an individual found guilty of heresy by the church, was to be handed over to the king's officers who *shall receive, and them before the people in a high place cause to be burnt, that such punishments may strike fear into the minds of others, whereby no such wicked doctrine and heretical and erroneous opinions against the Catholic faith, Christian law and determination of the holy church shall be sustained.* [17]

It was for the Church to define what was meant by heresy. Shortly after the passing of this Act, the Arundel Constitution (1408) so named after the reigning Archbishop of Canterbury, defined heresy in thirteen Articles, including:

Article 7. The translation of the text of Holy Scripture out of one tongue into another is a dangerous thing; ... therefore we enact and ordain that no one henceforth do by his own authority translate any text of Holy Scripture into the English tongue.

Article 9. Let no one presume to dispute of things determined by the Church either publicly, or privately.... Let him that asserts, teaches, preaches, or pertinaciously intimates the contrary incur the penalties of heresy. [18]

These Articles neatly foreshadow the forthcoming conflict between the authority of the Church and lay people, English Bible in hand, challenging that authority. The most important missing element in the Church of pre-Reformation times was the Bible as **the** authoritative source of teaching. John Wycliffe had translated it into English from Latin and his followers, the Lollards, copied parts by hand, which were passed from one to another and read in private. However, from 1408 this practice became dangerous.

At the peak of the hierarchy was the Pope, head of the Church and supreme governor of the kingdoms of earth. The Church had transformed itself into a power which every kingdom in Europe was expected to support. If any disobeyed, then the power of interdict fell on them. This power could shut the churches, suspend the sacraments surrounding birth, marriage and death, and withdraw from the hapless monarch all support from the Church and its loyal adherents. King John had been excommunicated in 1209 because he wished to appoint the next Archbishop of Canterbury against the wishes of the Pope. To keep his throne John found it needful to submit to the Pope, which he did in 1213. At the dawn of the Reformation this combination of spiritual and temporal power which the Church wielded had remained intact for nearly six hundred years.

The central teaching of the Roman Catholic Church in which Coverdale became a priest, was that good works, obedience to the Church, and a strictly observed round of duty were able to save the soul. Coverdale's good friend John Foxe, when writing his Book of Martyrs, described the orthodox religion of the day thus:

After the pope's catholic religion, a true Christian man is thus defined: first to be baptized in the Latin tongue, then confirmed by the bishop; after he be grown to years, then to come to church; to keep his fasting days; to be confessed of the priest; to do his penance; to hear mass; to fast the Lent; at Easter to take his rites; to set up candles before images; to creep to the cross; to take holy bread and holy water; to go on procession; to carry his palm and candle, and to take ashes; to pay his tithes; to go on pilgrimage; to buy pardons; to worship his Maker over the priest's head; to receive the pope as his supreme head and obey his laws; to have his beads, and to give to the high altar. To take orders if he will be a priest, to say his matins, to sing his mass; to keep his vow and not to marry; to be buried in the churchyard; to be rung for; to be sung for; to find a soul-priest, etc.

All which points being observed, who can deny but this is a devout man and a perfect Christian catholic; and sure to be saved as a true faithful child of the holy mother church. [19]

Coverdale and the other early Reformers, contrasted this teaching with the light they believed they had received from the gospel. *The gospel is not a corporal, but a spiritual kingdom; neither consisteth it in outward things, but a pure and faithful believing heart: and yet reacheth it throughout the whole world and amongst all nations. In the hearts of all faithful believers doth Christ reign through His Spirit, and there overcometh he the devil, sin and death.* [20]

Chapter 3

The dawn of the Reformation

But rise up, and stand upon thy feet, for therefore have I appeared unto thee, that I might ordain thee to be a minister and witness of it that thou hast seen, and that I will yet cause to appear unto thee. And I will deliver thee from the people and from the heathen, among whom I will now send thee, to open their eyes, that they may turn from the darkness unto the light, and from the power of the devil unto God, that they may receive forgiveness of sins, and the inheritance with them that are sanctified by faith in me. (Acts 26 Block C)

What was the Reformation?

There have been many attempts of recent years to explain the significance of the Reformation in terms of a social, political and cultural revolution. However, the core of this movement and of its early leaders was religious and spiritual. D'Aubigne describes it thus:

Those heavenly powers which had laid dormant in the church since the first ages of Christianity, awoke from their slumbers in the sixteenth century, and this awakening called the modern times into existence. The church was created anew, and from that regeneration flowed great developments of literature and science, of morality, liberty and industry. [1]

The Reformation was not so much a revolution in the modern sense but a return to the principles of the Primitive Christians in the early church; not a violent overthrow of the existing order or an upheaval in the way society was governed. It re-established the New Testament ideal of a relationship between the Creator and the creature, removing the priesthood which had grown between. *It is sufficient for a man to be contrite between God and his conscience, without confession made to a priest.* [2]

One of Coverdale's early translations into English was Henri Bullinger's *The Old Faith*. By way of introduction, Coverdale states that the new doctrine was that of the New Testament church. He emphasised two points that are of huge importance if we are to understand both his own life in particular and the Reformation in general.

I have here set forth this book: partly because it showeth the antiquity and ancient age of our Christian faith.... Now, because none other virtue can so apprehend the mercy of God, nor certify (assure) us so effectually of our salvation as this living faith doth, **therefore hath the Scripture imputed our justification before God only unto faith** *... without any other work or deed. This is the faith of Christ which all the Scriptures speak of. This is the faith without which it is impossible to please God. This is the faith whereby God purifieth our hearts, and whose end is salvation. This then is no new-fangled faith, no faith invented by man's brain, but even the same that God's Holy Spirit teacheth in the* **infallible truth of His scripture.** [3]

These two points were to be insisted on throughout by Coverdale and the other early Reformers. First, the Bible is the infallible truth of God. Secondly, justification is by faith only, and that while good works are a fruit of faith, works do not make a person right in the sight of God. Such principles undermined the very foundations of the Church from which they separated.

Writing during his second exile, Coverdale spoke severely: *Without the church, ye say, is no salvation. Now is it manifest, that there is a church of forward and wicked doers, which not only gather themselves together like roaring lions and cur dogs against Christ, but also make laws, ordinances and traditions against God's word; whereby though they boast never so much of God's service, yet all is to them in vain.* [4]

It was at Cambridge, so far as we can trace the Reformation back to its start in England, that this light first dawned among a group of students at that University. There were perhaps three influences which helped forward and encouraged them from 1521-25: the Lollards, the Renaissance and Martin Luther

The Lollards

The Lollards were followers of John Wycliffe who, using his mighty pen and great learning, provided the most serious threat to the Roman Catholic Church in the ages before the Reformation. His earlier writings against the monastic system and against transubstantiation prepared many for the struggles to come.

For many years too, a tax had been levied in England and elsewhere to support the Popes. In 1365, Urban V revived the claim on England for 1000 marks, with arrears from 1332 when the tax was last paid. Edward III laid the matter before Parliament who, on the advice and by the influence of Wycliffe, refused to pay. Wycliffe was emboldened to give this advice by his own enlightened views. *Many think,* said he, *if they give a penny to the pardoner, they shall be forgiven for breaking all God's commandments, and therefore they take no heed how they keep them.* Already, he said, *a third or more of England is in the hands of the Pope. There cannot be two temporal sovereigns in one country; either Edward is king or Urban is king. We make our choice. We accept Edward of England and refuse Urban of Rome.* [5] Parliament was greatly influenced by his writings and Edward III, the most powerful king of England between William I and Henry VIII, made him his chaplain.

Wycliffe Memorial at Lutterworth

In 1377 four Papal Bulls were issued against Wycliffe, the Pope fearing that increasing numbers both at court and among the common people were becoming 'tainted' with heresy. His later years, spent at Lutterworth, saw Wycliffe engaged in the most lasting monument of his life: the translation of the Scriptures into English. He had to translate from the Latin Vulgate, as Greek was so little known in western Europe at that time. The Scriptures had to be copied by hand in the absence of printing. Wycliffe's followers, the Lollards, went out into England and Scotland preaching and reading the Scriptures to the people. Wycliffe died in 1384. Against all expectation, he came to his grave in peace.

However, Henry IV, aided by the clergy, soon began to stamp on the Lollards. The Lollard movement was quickly driven underground, where it remained from one generation to the next until the Reformation. Small parts of Wycliffe's Bible were copied out by hand and read to small groups where opportunity arose People met in houses and barns, especially in the Midlands and South-east, but also as far from Lutterworth as to Scotland, to read the Scriptures, pray and listen to the occasional itinerant preacher. When the teaching of Luther began to arrive in England and in Scotland after 1520, Tunstall, the bishop of London wrote to Erasmus: *It is no question of some pernicious novelty. It is only that new arms are being added to the great band of Wycliffe heretics.* [6]

When Coverdale and others were scattered from the universities, it was such groups as the Lollards who often provided the nucleus for their congregations and who avidly purchased both Bibles and the works of Luther. Derek Wilson states the case thus:

There was no Lollard creed or Lollard priesthood or Lollard hierarchy. What we are dealing with is a loose network of people who had discovered a secret and were trying to build their lives upon it. The exclusive knowledge they shared was that God revealed himself directly to his people via the Scriptures and without any need for clerical intermediaries. [7]

The Renaissance

To this picture must be added the Renaissance – a rebirth of learning, which pre-dated and helped forward the Reformation. It began in the city states of Northern Italy, sandwiched as they were between the Papal States to the south, and the Holy Roman Empire which governed Germany to the north. As the Saracens increasingly overran the centres of Greek learning in eastern Europe, and particularly after the fall of Constantinople in 1453, scholars began to move to western Europe, bringing with them the ancient texts of Christianity and learning in Greek and Hebrew.

A key figure in the Renaissance was Erasmus. In 1516 Erasmus, who had been working and teaching at Cambridge from 1509-14, produced his own Greek New Testament alongside a Latin translation. It involved significant changes from the Latin Vulgate, not least in the translation of the Greek word *matanoia* as repentance and not penance. Erasmus based his Greek New Testament on the manuscripts which had been unlocked by the migrating Greek scholars. His New Testament went through five editions in his lifetime, and was the basis of the Stephens Greek edition of 1555 on which both the Geneva and later the King James Versions of the English Bible were based. Erasmus set out clearly his motives:

But one thing the facts cry out, and it can be clear, as they say, even to a blind man, that often through the translator's clumsiness or inattention the Greek has been wrongly rendered; often the true and genuine reading has been corrupted by ignorant scribes, which we see happen every day, or altered by scribes who are half-taught and half-asleep. [8]

Such outspoken criticism was also directed by Erasmus at other aspects of the Roman Catholic Church. He was unsparing in his views on the luxury, superstition and ignorance of many in high places in that church. At this time the Roman Catholic church could boast its antiquity, its wealth and the laws of both England and Scotland buttressing its position. But it was quickly losing its hold on the affections of the people, especially in the hands of a greedy and all-powerful cleric such as Wolsey.

It is important though to distinguish between the Renaissance and the Reformation. Erasmus broke with Luther in 1525 over the doctrines of predestination and justification by faith only and died a Roman Catholic. More and Fisher, both leading scholars in the same tradition, were executed by Henry VIII, dying Roman Catholics. They were avid heresy hunters during their time in power, hunting down with great cruelty both Lollards and Lutherans. Other Renaissance scholars such as Bishops Lee, Longland and Tunstall all conformed to Henry's Anglican church after the split with Rome, but had little sympathy with the Reformation and Protestant teaching. It is also true that the Renaissance was about more than religion, and is remembered today for the way it began to unlock the arts and science.

The thirst for learning encouraged by the Renaissance coincided with the invention of printing. In 1454 Gutenberg, only months ahead of rivals in other centres, turned the first press. Caxton was the first printer in England in 1475 and Myllar in Scotland in 1507. Now 1000 copies per day of any book or pamphlet could come off the press, fuelling a huge rise in literacy and more consistency in written English. It took time for books to begin to sell, but by the 1520s there was an explosion of printing. Luther was the first writer who harnessed this new invention to reach large audiences. Most importantly, the Bible, translated into local languages, became widely available. Luther's first New Testament sold

5,000 copies in the first two weeks and went through many editions. Here was a single volume, against which the doctrines and practices of the Church could be measured, and that by ordinary people.

Old printing press now housed in The British Library. Printing changed little between its invention and the C19th.

The influence of Luther

It is highly significant that the dawn of the Reformation in England was some five years behind Germany, and coincided with the time when Luther's writings began to circulate around Europe. Luther's place in the Europe-wide Reformation is beyond doubt. He was a prolific writer, producing many books per year for over thirty years. The reformed German churches began to be called 'Lutheran' at a very early stage.

His public ministry was a reflection of his early experience in the Austin Friars' cell at Erfurt. Here, he tells us, he felt God's anger against him for sin. Being trained to think he could merit heaven by his works, he set about the salvation of his soul in earnest, with all the power of a keen and eager spirit. *I was indeed a pious monk,* he wrote to Duke George of Saxony, *and followed the rules of my order more strictly than I can express. If ever monk could obtain heaven by his monkish works, I should certainly have been entitled to it. Of this, all the friars who have known me can testify. If it had continued much longer, I should have carried my mortifications even to death, by means of my watchings, prayers, reading and other labours.* [9]

In this state a fellow monk gave Luther a Bible. This Book became his constant companion. But Luther still had many struggles before his deliverance from the chains in which he was held. D'Aubigne writes: *One day, as he lay overwhelmed with despair, an aged monk entered his cell and addressed a few words of comfort to him. Luther opened his heart to him and made known the fears by which he was tormented. …. Leading him back to that Apostles' Creed which Luther had learned in early childhood at the school at Mansfeldt, the aged monk repeated this article with kind good nature: 'I believe in the forgiveness of sins.' These simple words, which the pious brother pronounced with sincerity in this decisive moment, diffused great consolation in Luther's heart.* [10]

In 1508 Luther, at the invitation of Frederick the Wise, Elector of Saxony, became Professor at the University of Wittenberg, at the centre of the Reformation which was to sweep through northern Germany. His break with Rome came in a series of steps between 1517-20.

First was the posting of his ninety-five theses to the church door at Wittenberg in October 1517 and their diffusion through northern Europe. Pope Leo X wanted money to rebuild St Peter's Church in Rome on as grand a scale as Solomon's Temple. Where was the money to come from? Not from war-torn Italy, where the kings of France and Spain vied for mastery. He turned his eyes to the German territory of the Holy Roman Empire. And so Tetzel was sent with indulgences which, for sums of money, would give a passport into heaven. Luther's theses were his reply to this trade. His indignation was raised especially by the way the poor, who could hardly find bread to feed their families, were parting with the necessities of life to these teachers who offered them forgiveness of sins for money.

Statue of Martin Luther at Wittenberg

Thesis 27: They preach mere human follies who maintain that as soon as the money rattles into the strongbox, the soul flies out of purgatory.

Thesis 32: Those who fancy themselves sure of salvation by indulgences will go to perdition along with those who teach them so.

At this stage, Luther had no thought of separating from the Church, rather to reform it, and in 1518, he wrote to the Pope, to try to make him aware that the avarice of the priests and the whole trade in indulgences, had brought the Church into disrepute.

Chiefly by the powerful influence of the Elector of Saxony, the Church arranged several disputations with Luther over the succeeding two years. These centred around such key questions as the authority of the Church or the authority of the Bible. The final step was the disputation with Dr Eck. This took place at Leipzig in 1519 and centred around the headship of the Church. Eck insisted that the head of the Church on earth was the Pope; Luther that it was Christ. The course taken in this disputation convinced Luther to throw off the authority of the Pope. The result was Luther's book, *The Reformation of Christianity,* written in 1520. The Papal Bull of excommunication which was then issued against Luther completed the separation. Luther's fame increased and his books not only flew round Germany, but found a ready audience in other countries, including England.

This dispute also brought Luther into conflict with Charles V. The death of Maximillian the Holy Roman Emperor in January 1519, meant the seven German Electors had to decide on his replacement. The most important of these Electors was Frederick of Saxony, Luther's employer. By agreement of the whole number of Electors, the throne was given to twenty-year-old Charles V, King of Spain. Charles, beset by war with France, with the Turks encroaching on his vast kingdoms to the east, and beholden to the Elector of Saxony, summoned Luther to Worms in

1521 to answer for his heresies. Luther obeyed the summons. Asked to recant, he refused. *Since your Majesty asks for a plain answer, I will give you one without horns or teeth.... I neither can nor will recant, since it is neither right nor safe to act against conscience. God help me, Amen.* [11] Over the next 25 years the attention and energies of Charles V were absorbed by wars, leaving the putting down of the German Reformation until after the 1546 death of Luther. By the time the Emperor set out in earnest to suppress heresy, he was too late. The movement had grown too big to be easily destroyed by either Church or ruler.

On the way back from Worms Luther was captured and taken into friendly captivity at Wartburg Castle, where he stayed for ten months. It was in this solitary place, unable to preach or invigorate his friends by his presence, that he turned his attention in 1522 to giving the people of Germany the New Testament in their own language. He was greatly helped in this work by Philip Melancthon, a notable Greek scholar who by this time had arrived at his side. They enjoyed a close friendship which endured until Luther's death.

Beginnings in England

The teachings of Luther were being passed from hand to hand in small quantities in England, but there was no sign of what was to come. The first half of Henry VIII's reign had seen little change in religious belief and practice. He was married in 1509, the year he came to the throne, to Catherine of Aragon, a Spanish Roman Catholic noblewoman. In 1521 Henry was awarded by the Pope the title *Defender of the Faith* for his book against Luther (probably written on his behalf by Sir Thomas More).

Far from the centre of power in England, the same light which had instructed the heart of Luther began to dawn among a few Cambridge students such as Coverdale, Frith, Bilney and Latimer. One of the first to reject the Church was Thomas Bilney, an oppressed and serious youth. The priests could do him no good. His fasting and penances emptied his purse, wasted his body and darkened his mind. He was searching for peace of mind and peace with God, but could find none. One day, a copy of Erasmus's Greek New Testament coming to hand, with fear and trembling, he took it up into his room. He says:

I also, a miserable sinner, before I came unto Christ, had spent all that I had on ignorant physicians... so that there was but small strength left in me, small store of money, and very little understanding. For they appointed me fastings, watchings, buying of pardons and masses; in all which things, as I now understand, they sought rather their own gain than the salvation of my sick and languishing soul. But at last I heard speak of Jesus, even when the New Testament was first set forth by Erasmus... And at the first reading, as I well remember, I chanced upon this sentence of Paul (O most sweet and comfortable sentence to my soul): 'It is a true saying and worthy of all men to be embraced, that Christ Jesus came into the world to save sinners, of whom I am chief and principal'. This one sentence, through God's instruction and inward working, which I did not then perceive, did so exhilarate my heart, being before wounded with guilt of my sins, and being almost in despair, that immediately I felt a marvellous comfort and quietness, insomuch that my bruised bones leaped for joy. [12]

This testimony of Bilney expresses the spiritual foundation of the Reformation. He began to assemble his friends and to expound his Greek Testament. His hand was soon strengthened by the coming of William Tyndale to Cambridge, and then by a young scholar John Frith. To these three must be added Robert Barnes, the Prior of the Austin Friary in Cambridge. Barnes had already studied the Greek New Testament closely, and preached against the worldliness of the church. However, Bilney took him and instructed him more clearly in the gospel. Others soon began to gather around them, meeting to read their New Testaments and Luther's writings in the White Horse Inn, commonly called 'Little Germany' in reference to the influence of Luther. Collinson speaks of *the translators, the twenty-five Cambridge martyrs, and the ninety Marion exiles from Cambridge who almost monopolize the history of the early Protestant tradition in this country.* [13]

Another of these scholars was Coverdale. John Bale, later a bishop in Ireland during the reign of Edward VI, who knew Coverdale well, gave this description of him: *He was a young man of friendly upright nature, and very gentle spirit. And when the Church of England was revived he was one of the first to make a pure profession of Christ. Other men gave themselves in part, he gave himself wholly to propagating the truth of Christ's gospel. The spirit of God is in some a vehement wind overturning mountains and rocks but in him it is a still small voice comforting wavering hearts. His style is charming and gentle, flowing limpidly along, it moves, instructs and delights.* [14]

While we have no record of the circumstances surrounding Coverdale's conversion, we can piece together from his writings the substance of the change which brought him out of the Austin Friary into the uncertain and hazardous life of an early Reformer. In his *Fruitful Lessons* he describes a change in spiritual condition which no doubt reflected his own experience.

When the poor sinner through the preaching of the Holy Ghost heareth his wicked and sinful life, (for the Holy Ghost rebuketh the world of sin,) he beginneth to know himself a sinner, and to be displeased, repentant and sorry for his sins; he considereth also, that he is well worthy of eternal punishment and damnation: by means whereof, through the multitude and greatness of his sins, he utterly despairs in his own power and righteousness and eternal salvation.

But therewithal he heareth also, that Christ, by reason of his sins, came down from heaven, and died for him on the cross, washed away all his sins in his blood, hath reconciled him with God, made him God's child, and an eternal inheritor of His kingdom; and this he steadfastly believeth. I pray you, doth not such a man's heart leap for joy, when he heareth, that through Christ he is discharged of all the sins that so sore pressed him [15]

Plaque in King's College, Cambridge

The Friary of which Coverdale was a member took its name from Augustine of Hippo (AD 354-430), though founded 700 years after his death. Clearly Coverdale knew his writings well, and often quoted them: *Follow Augustine's counsel then, and boast not of man's merits; but let the grace of God which reigneth through Jesus Christ have all the pre-eminence.* [16]   In the prologue to his 1535 Bible, Coverdale made clear that in Augustine's time, the Bible was still being translated from one language to another, and people could study it in their own tongue to their benefit.   He laments that this changed soon thereafter. *As soon as the Bible was cast aside... then began everyone of his own head to write whatsoever came into his own brain ... and so grew the darkness of men's traditions.* [17]

Another, brought out of 'the darkness of men's traditions', who began to gather in 'Little Germany' in these early days was Coverdale's friend and fellow priest Hugh Latimer.   In 1524 a zealous and fervent Roman Catholic, Latimer, inflamed by the daring heresies of Luther and others, felt inclined to strike a blow for the Papacy.   He was asked to deliver a Latin discourse before the Cambridge fellows.   His chosen subject was Luther's friend Philip Melancthon, one who dared to advance the heresy that the church fathers had to be interpreted by the light of the Holy Scriptures.   His discourse made a great sensation.   At last here was a doctor worthy to combat the Lutheran teachers!   However, one of his audience thought differently.   Bilney *was a trier out of Satan's subtleties, called of God to detect the bad money that the enemy was circulating through the church.*[18] Bilney asked Latimer, in his role as a priest, to hear confession.   Kneeling before the unsuspecting Latimer, Bilney told him simply of his anguish of soul, his efforts to remove his guilt, and the unprofitable remedies of the priests.   He then spoke of the peace of God which filled his heart when he was given the spirit of adoption to believe that Christ was the lamb of God which taketh away the sin of the world.   Latimer gives his own testimony of this remarkable interview. *From that time forward I began to smell the word of God, and forsook the doctors of the schools and other such fooleries.* [19] Thus Latimer began to strengthen the hands of Bilney, Coverdale and the small group of Lutherans who taught publicly that penance, intercession of the saints, ceremonies of the church and the whole structure of works, could not freely justify sinners. Only the finished work of Christ on the cross was enough. No longer was the fruit of Christianity to be creeping to the cross or the offering of candles before shrines, but visiting the sick, relieving the poor and teaching repentance toward God and faith toward the Lord Jesus Christ.

The Reformation spreads to Oxford and beyond

In 1525 the Reformation began to move forward at Oxford too, through the instrumentality of Cardinal Wolsey! He had grand plans to create Cardinal College which would be a lasting memorial to his worth. He recruited ten top scholars from Cambridge. At least two, John Clark and John Frith, had embraced Lutheran teaching. Frith excelled in Mathematics, but found in Holy Scripture learning of a new kind. *Mere study is sufficient to impress the theories of mathematics on our minds; but this science of God meets with a resistance in man that necessitates the intervention of a Divine power. Christianity is a regeneration.* [20]

The key figure though was John Clark, appointed Professor of Divinity at Oxford. We have an account written by one Oxford student, showing the spread of the gospel under his preaching and teaching: *Now there were at that time in Oxford many graduates and scholars whom God had called to the knowledge of His Holy Word, which all resorted unto Master Clark's lectures in divinity at all times they might, and when they might not conveniently come, I was by Master Clark appointed to resort unto every one of them weekly, and to know what doubts they had in any place of the Scriptures; that from him, they might have the true understanding of the same, which exercises did me most good and profit, to the understanding of Holy Scriptures.* [21]

Alarm was spreading among the authorities at the appearance of Tyndale's New Testament. By the time they began to suspect heresy in 1526-28, and tried to take steps to suppress it, there was a band of Reformers at both universities and the number of earnest students of the Scriptures was increasing daily. The steps taken by the bishops scattered these students, but rather than snuff out heresy, it caused it to spread more widely. At Oxford, from February to August of 1528, Frith, Clark and others were imprisoned in the cellars under Cardinal College, and given nothing but salt fish to eat. Three of them, one of whom was John Clark, died before the others were released. Many suspected of Lutheranism left Oxford.

At Cambridge, the Bishop of Ely took the first step to suppress heresy by banning Latimer from preaching in the pulpits in the University or town of Cambridge. Coverdale's friend and mentor Robert Barnes, as Prior of the Austin Friary, invited Latimer to his pulpit, which was not under the bishop's authority, while he Barnes preached in a town pulpit. However, Barnes' zeal outran his discretion, and he used his sermon to attack Wolsey. It would seem at this time that his opposition to the corruptions in the church was more pronounced than his Lutheranism.

Barnes ran into serious trouble as a result of his pulpit utterances. A sergeant-at-arms was sent up from Wolsey in London to arrest him and to make search for Luther's books. But a sympathetic official sent word privately to some thirty suspected persons who, having been warned, hid their books. Barnes, with Coverdale in attendance, was arrested and taken to London, to appear before Cardinal Wolsey.

Wolsey appeared in all his pomp before the intimidated Barnes. *Do you not know that I am Legatus de latere, and that I am able to dispense in all matters concerning religion within this realm, as much as the Pope may?* [21a]   At first Barnes seemed inclined to hold his ground.   He answered, *I thank your Grace for your good will; I will stick to the Holy Scripture, and to God's book, according to the simple talent that God hath lent me.   Well,* said he, *thou shalt have thy learning tried to the uttermost, and thou shalt have the law.*

On the Saturday he came again before them into the chapter-house, and there remained till five o'clock at night; and after long disputations and threatening, they called him, to know whether he would recant or burn. He was then in a great agony, and thought rather to burn than to recant. But then was he sent again to have the counsel of Gardiner, a fellow student from Cambridge, and others, and they persuaded him rather to recant than to burn, because (they said) he should do more in time to come; and with many other persuasions they weakened his resolve.   We have a vivid account of the occasion which occurred on Shrove Sunday 1526.

In the morning they were all ready, by their hour appointed, in Paul's church, the church being so full that no man could get in. The cardinal had a scaffold made on the top of the stairs for himself, with six-and-thirty abbots, mitred priors, and bishops, and he, in his whole pomp, mitred, sat there enthroned, his chaplains and spiritual doctors in gowns of damask and satin, and he himself in purple.   And there was a new pulpit erected on the top of the stairs also, for the bishop of Rochester to preach against Luther and Dr. Barnes; and great baskets full of books standing before them, within the rails, which were commanded, after the great fire was made before the rood, there to be burned; and these heretics, after the sermon, to go thrice about the fire, and to cast in their faggots. Now, while the sermon was a doing, Dr. Barnes was commanded to kneel down, and ask forgiveness of God, of the catholic church and of the cardinal's Grace: and, after that, he was commanded, to declare, that he was more charitably handled than he deserved, or was worthy; his heresies were so horrible and so detestable. And once again he kneeled down on his knees, desiring of the people forgiveness and to pray for him. [22]

Barnes was then committed to the Fleet prison but after a few weeks released as a free prisoner to the Austin Friars in London. He was, however, quickly having second thoughts about his recantation. Copies of Tyndale's New Testament were circulating in London, and we gather that Barnes was soon selling them. One copy he sold to a group of Lollards, who shortly were to have Coverdale preaching in their midst. *An Essex Lollard, John Tyball and his friends from Bumpstead visited Barnes in his chamber, and found other callers including a London merchant, busily reading the new book. The men from Essex made themselves known to Barnes ... showed him tattered Lollard manuscripts of the Scriptures, as of the four evangelists and certain epistles of Peter and Paul. Which books Barnes did little regard, saying they were not to be compared with the new printed Testament in English.* [22a]

Coverdale leaves the Friary

At the start of these troubles, in 1527, Coverdale took the important decision to leave behind his monastic life and vows, and to go about preaching the gospel. His first letter which has survived is to Thomas Cromwell, dated May Day 1527, and is signed 'Brother' Myles Coverdale; it is written from the 'Augustins'. The second, dated 27th August 1527 is simply from Cambridge, signed with no title of 'brother', and states a willingness to come to London. Many others of the Cambridge group also had scattered. Writing to his Devon friends twenty-six years later, after he was ordered to London with the other bishops at the start of Mary's reign, he wrote:

How horrible things are in the mass book I learned many years ago, which as I utterly abhor, and all other idolatry, superstition, witchcrafts, extortions, filthiness, sodomitish chastity, pilgrimages, images, etc, even so my conscience and I, upon the most sure grounds of God's most holy commandments, God's fatherly promises, and most undoubted ensamples and practices of his old holy and ancient children, are at a sure point and steadfastly determined never to return to Egypt, never to kiss the calf, never to meddle with my old vomit, never to be defiled again with strange meats, never to worship Nebuchadnezzar's golden image, never to receive the beast's mark, never to shake hands with the devil, never to take of him wages or livery, and to be short, never to forsake, refuse or recant the word of life. [23] This letter breathes the absolute determination he had to leave behind the practices of monastic life and the religion in which he had lived for so long. He had been over twelve years an ordained priest in the Roman Catholic Church.

He was soon preaching in and around London. Preaching at Steeple Bumpstead on the Essex/Suffolk border, where there were a number of Lollards, he was the instrument in the conversion of one Thomas Topley. Topley, and his brother, had both been members of the Austin Friary in the next village of Stoke by Clare. Both were convinced to give up their monastic life. When Topley was examined by the Bishop of London, as to why he had forsaken his order of the Austin Friars, he said he had read Wycliffe's Wicket, which had greatly troubled his mind as it *did make the sacrament of Christ's body, in form of bread, but a remembrance of Christ's death. That trouble continued until I heard Miles Coverdale preach*, which cleared his mind that this Lollard doctrine was Scriptural. He went on to describe to the Bishop how he *was walking in the field at Bumpstead, with Miles Coverdale, late friar of the same order, going in the habit of a secular priest, who had preached the fourth Sunday in Lent at Bumpstead .... This Miles said and did hold, that it was sufficient for a man to be contrite for his sins betwixt God and his conscience, without confession made to a priest. At the same sermon, made by the said Miles Coverdale at Bumpstead, I heard him preach against worshipping of images in the church, saying and preaching that men in no wise should honour or worship them.* [24]

The Parish Church at Steeple Bumpstead, a church where Coverdale preached after leaving the priesthood.

This congregation of Lollards must have been fairly big, as some forty members in the Steeple Bumpstead group got into serious trouble with Stokesley, the Bishop of London 1531-32, and were by him imprisoned and examined, no doubt with threat of fire. Their recantations in the Bishop's register were copied out and summarised by Foxe. He says of them:

So great was the trouble of those times, that it would overcharge any story to recite the names of all them that during those bitter days before the coming of queen Anne (Boleyn), *either were driven out of the realm, or were cast out from their goods and houses, or were brought to open shame by abjuration.... Such watch and narrow search was used, such ways were taken by force of oath to make one detect another so subtly that scarcely any good man could or did escape their hands, but either his name was known, or else his person was taken. Yet nevertheless, so mightily the power of God's gospel did work in the hearts of good men, that the number of them did nothing lessen for all this violence or policy of the adversaries but rather increased.* [25]

That Coverdale felt he would have to leave preaching in England for translation work in exile is suggested by a letter he wrote during that year to Thomas Cromwell, a rising public servant in London, and secretary to Cardinal Wolsey. By this time Cromwell had moved into a home rented from the Austin Friary in London, and evidently knew Coverdale. Coverdale wrote to him as follows:

Most singular good master, ...for the fervent zeal that you have to virtue and to godly study, I humbly desire and beseech your goodness of your gracious help. Now I begin to taste of Holy Scriptures: now, honour be to God! I am set to the most sweet smell of holy letters, with the godly savour of holy and ancient doctors, unto whose knowledge I cannot attain without diversity of books, as is not unknown to your most excellent wisdom. Nothing in the world I desire but books, as concerning my learning: once had, I do not doubt but Almighty God shall perform that in me, which he of his most plentiful favour and grace hath begun.[26]

Coverdale's yearning for a greater field of usefulness was to be granted him sooner than he realised. He had seen at close hand the treatment of Barnes and others. This clearly made a great impression on Coverdale. If he stayed in England, he could soon expect the same treatment: recant or burn. Henry VIII made clear his own commands, reacting to the increased number of Tyndale New Testaments finding their way into England. *We, with the deliberate advice of the most reverend fathers of the spirituality, have determined the said untrue translation to be burned, with further sharp correction and punishment against readers of the same.* [28] Knowing Coverdale's gentle and tractable disposition, would he hold out when his friends had not? On the other hand, by fleeing into a life of exile, might he do some good to the cause of the Reformation in England from beyond the seas?

The works of Luther, the light beginning to spread in England, and above all the introduction of the English New Testament began to increase the alarm of the authorities. Tyndale had facilitated the printing of 3,000 copies at Worms, and others, seeing the profit in the trade, were pirating them in Antwerp. A steady flow of Lutheran books was finding a receptive market, not just in Oxford and Cambridge, but also in London and other centres of Lollard strength. Leading the clamp-down against the Lutherans were Cardinal Wolsey, Bishop Tunstall and Sir Thomas More. A small sign of the times was that Tunstall already was burning Tyndale's New Testament at Paul's Cross, claiming he had found over 2000 errors therein.

The prisons in London and Colchester began to overflow with Lutherans from 1528-31. Several who held firm were burned at the stake, beginning with Thomas Hitton at Maidstone in Kent. This led to a strongly-worded exchange between More and Tyndale. More concludes his account of Hitton by writing: *He had learned his false faith and heresies from Tyndale's holy books, and now the spirit of error and lying hath taken his wretched soul with him straight from the short fire to the fire everlasting. And this is Thomas Hitton the devil's stinking martyr.* [28] Some ten to twelve more were burned at the stake over the next two or three years, including Bilney and Frith, the most fervent preachers among the former Cambridge students. Stokesley replaced Tunstall as Bishop of London in 1530, and was even hotter against heresy, until the king's great matter reined him in.

From Coverdale's name being mentioned in so public a manner as a preacher in the Lollard group at Steeple

Bumpstead, clearly he could no longer stay in England, unless he too would share the troubles which had come upon the Lutherans. John Hooker tells us that he left England *very straightly pursued by the bishops.* [29] William Tyndale was busy with translation work, and arranged for Coverdale to meet him in Hamburg.[30]

Chapter Four

First exile. The 1535 Coverdale Bible

And for so much as thou hast known holy scripture of a child, the same is able to make thee wise unto salvation through the faith in Christ Jesus. For all scripture given by inspiration of God, is profitable to teach, to improve, to amend, and to instruct in righteousness, that a man of God may be perfect, and prepared unto all good works. (2Tim 3 block A)

Exile

William Tyndale had by 1528 been abroad for several years, in *poverty, exile, absence from friends, hunger, thirst, cold and the great danger wherewith I am everywhere encompassed.* [1]   Having first asked Tunstall, Bishop of London, for his agreement to sponsor the translation of the Bible into English, and having been refused, it was clear to Tyndale that, there being no place of safety in England, he would need to work from abroad.   But where?

Tyndale in 1526 was in the German city of Worms.   In that city he issued the first printed English New Testament. Tyndale was the first to harness the new discoveries by Erasmus and others of Hebrew and Greek learning, and to present them to an English readership. His scholarship was equalled by the clarity and forcefulness of his English.   His New Testament contains many memorable phrases which have come down to the present.   Some 85% of the King James Version New Testament is reckoned to have come straight from Tyndale's two editions – a monumental achievement when one considers he was a fugitive, alone and with no certain dwelling place. By 1528, Tyndale had moved to Antwerp, where his *Parable of Wicked Mammon* was written, based on Luke 16. The book taught that justification is by faith, not by works. Apart from his New Testament translations this was Tyndale's greatest influence on the Reformation. However, the reaction among the English authorities was to step up the level of heresy-hunting abroad as well as at home. In June 1528, Cardinal Wolsey instructed the English ambassador to the Low Countries to demand from the Regent, Charles V's sister, the most prominent of the English 'heretics' for trial. An English merchant, Richard Herman, was caught and thrown into prison, but Tyndale, recognising that Antwerp was unsafe, fled to Hamburg where by appointment he met Coverdale.

The north German states were becoming safer under Luther's influence, but did not offer easy access to England, neither did they have many English residents. Foxe tells us that Tyndale suffered shipwreck on the way, with the loss of all his papers. No doubt the coming of Coverdale to join with his work was some consolation for his losses. For Coverdale, it would be an excellent opportunity to serve an apprenticeship under one of the most gifted scholars of his day. In Hamburg they lodged with a widow, mistress Margaret Van Emersen, until late in 1529, while Tyndale retranslated the Pentateuch (the first five books of the Bible) with Coverdale's help. However, at the end of 1529, with the plague now having reached Hamburg, Tyndale and Coverdale left the town.

The movements of the men thereafter are not clear as they were involved in a perilous activity and of necessity kept a low profile; it is thought that they resided in Antwerp for much of the remainder of the first exile. By the end of 1529, with

Henry VIII's divorce beginning to dominate English public life, and with the fall of Wolsey, the spotlight on Antwerp faded. Richard Herman was released after some eight months in prison and the case against him dropped; by the end of the year it was safe for Tyndale and Coverdale to return.

Nevertheless, the safety was only relative. Any Bible translation work at that time was bound to bring danger on the head of its authors. The peril with which they were surrounded is shown by an interview described by Steven Vaughan, Henry VIII's factor in the Low Countries. He was instructed by Thomas Cromwell, in 1531, to find Tyndale and persuade him to return to England. Enquiring in vain in the various towns of Hamburg, Marburg and Frankfurt, he was contacted by a messenger who conducted him to a field outside Antwerp, to meet a stranger who could give him information about Tyndale's whereabouts. The stranger was Tyndale himself. Tyndale was deeply moved by the offer, and said he would return to England within two days, even if it meant his death, **once the king gave to his people the Bible in English.**

Coverdale in Antwerp

Antwerp had a sizeable English community at that time and many exiles found a home there, despite the Low Countries (today's Belgium and Netherlands) being under Spanish rule. As the foremost port and largest town in the Low Countries, Antwerp was one of the wealthiest cities of Europe. Its wealth was a product of trade: in spices and other valuables from the Spanish and Portuguese empires, in minerals from Germany and wool from England.

C16th Map of Antwerp by kind permission of the executors of the late Lewis Lupton. The English House was two blocks east of the central church, and the English Quay at the north end of the city on the river Scheldt.

Merchants from many countries had offices there and traded in the Bourse (market). As it was dangerous to ship gold and silver around Europe, increasingly, wealthier merchants set up banks to facilitate trade. English commerce was very important to the prosperity of Antwerp, employing large numbers, especially handling the clothtrade. Wool was England's biggest export at this time and much of the trade went through Antwerp, where the wool was dyed and finished. It is estimated that 20,000 were employed in English trade at Antwerp. [2] The Company of Merchant Adventurers looked after this flow of goods. They were based in London and represented the interests of English traders in Antwerp from the 'English House', their Antwerp headquarters. These merchants had a degree of diplomatic immunity, partly because of their ability to lend money to kings and princes, and partly by the charters they had negotiated over the years with the rulers of the Low Countries. A constant flow of ships docked at the English quay on the riverside.

Antwerp was also a significant centre of printing. Stephen Alford tells us that between 1500 and 1540, there were sixty-six printing firms in the town and that *Antwerp was the largest producer of Protestant literature in English before the 1540s.* [3] Quoting a German source, Mozley tells us that Coverdale earned his living as a proof-reader to the printer Martin de Keyser. [4] No doubt this arrangement suited both parties, as scholars of Coverdale's stature would rarely be available to printers in the Low Countries.

It was here Coverdale began his translation work, beginning in 1534 with an English translation from Campensis' Latin version of the Psalms. Campensis, who died in 1528, had been Professor of Hebrew at the University of Louvain. The preface is typical of Coverdale's style. *Though I durst not be so foolish as to put forth any text, because I have not such understanding in the three languages as is needful for him that should well and truly translate any text of Scripture, yet because I myself have found such fruit and comfort in this little book, I could not be so uncharitable unto my natural country as to withhold them the fruit of it.* (Coverdale's preface to *A Paraphrase upon all the Psalms of David*.)

In 1534, John Rogers came to Antwerp as Chaplain to the Merchant Adventurers. Foxe tells us that there he fell into company with Tyndale and Coverdale and, it would seem, was converted by their labours and so joined with them in their translation work. *In conferring with them in the Scriptures, he came to great knowledge in the gospel of God, insomuch that he cast off the heavy yoke of popery, perceiving it to be impure and filthy idolatry and joined himself with them two in the most painful and profitable labour of translating the Bible into the English tongue.* [5]

The perils surrounding these first translators were emphasised by the betrayal of Tyndale in the spring of 1535 in Antwerp. Lured out of the English House by one whom he had befriended, the Emperor's men were lying in wait. Taking him the fifteen miles to Vilvoorde, near Brussels, the centre of administration of the Emperor's government of the Low Countries, he was thrown into prison out of reach of his friends. Despite the efforts of Thomas Cromwell and the outrage of the English merchants at this breach of their diplomatic immunity, he languished in prison for sixteen months before being taken out, strangled and burnt. By the time of his arrest, not only had he reprinted a second edition of the New Testament but was half-way through the Old Testament. His death, a triumph to his enemies, was no doubt a real blow to Coverdale and Rogers.

1535 Coverdale Bible

Coverdale's Bible completed Tyndale's labours after his friend and mentor was seized. The result was the first printed Bible in English. A major problem was his lack of Tyndale's insight into the languages of the Bible: Hebrew and Greek. This problem he acknowledged plainly and openly at the start of his Preface to the reader: *To help me herein, I have had sundry translations, not only in Latin, but also of the Douche* (German) *interpreters: whom (because of their singular gifts and special diligence in the Bible) I have been the more glad to follow for the most part, according as I was required.* (Preface to 1535 Bible).

It has been deduced that Coverdale's 'sundry translations' were five in number:

- Tyndale's English New Testament, Pentateuch and the Prophecy of Jonah
- Luther's German Bible
- The Zurich Bible produced by Zwingli and his team
- Pagninus' Latin Old Testament of 1528. This translation was by one of the best Hebraists of his day who had spent thirty years on the work
- Jerome's Vulgate dating back to the fourth century AD

Coverdale's New Testament and Pentateuch (plus the book of Jonah) were light revisions of Tyndale. The epistles of James and Jude in his Bible are Tyndale's version almost word-for-word. The rest of the Bible from Joshua to Malachi, Tyndale had begun to translate and his work on Joshua to 2 Chronicles surfaced in the Matthews Bible two years later. This suggests John Rogers had been entrusted with these papers, and that Coverdale did not have access to them.

Writing in May 2020, Hine suggests, based on an intensive study of the book of Ruth, that *the 1534 Zurich Bible had a unique position among Coverdale's sources.* [6] This, perhaps, does not apply to the Psalms, where Luther's genius in translating poetry made his German Bible more important. I tend to the view that Coverdale used all of the versions available to him, but especially Tyndale's, to support but not determine his own translation. He was a scholar of sufficient stature to make his own decisions as to when to follow and when to vary from other translators.

In the prologue to this Bible Coverdale suggests that he himself was somewhat slow to put his hand to this great undertaking. *Considering how excellent knowledge and learning an interpreter of Scripture ought to have in the tongues, and pondering also mine own insufficiency therein, and how weak I am to perform the office of translator, I was the more loath to meddle with this work.* (Preface to 1535 Bible) Coverdale began his work some months before Tyndale's arrest, and finished it while Tyndale awaited execution in the prison at Vilvoorde. *Notwithstanding, when I considered how great pity it was that we should want it so long, and called to my remembrance the adversity of them which were not only of ripe knowledge, but would also with all their hearts have performed that which they began, … I was the more bold to take it in hand.* This suggests

Walls of Jericho falling – Woodcut from 1535 Bible

Tyndale's imprisonment was a spur to Coverdale in his work.

Coverdale's Bible was large (folio) size, printed in two columns and with over 120 woodcuts of Bible scenes. He followed Luther who, in his 1534 German Bible, had for the first time put the Apocrypha between the Testaments as a separate section. His reason, Coverdale tells us, was: *These books, good reader, which are called the Apocrypha, are not judged among the doctors to be of like reputation with the other Scriptures.... And the chief cause thereof is this: there be many places in them, that seem to be repugnant unto the open and manifest truth in other books of the Bible.* (1535 Preface)

Many writers have accepted uncritically the judgment of C.S.Lewis, who remarked that of the translators of the sixteenth century Coverdale *shows like a rowing-boat among battleships.* [7] However, that is neither fair nor accurate. Coverdale was a scholar who took great care to convey in clear dignified English the meaning of the text and, importantly, knew his own limitations in Hebrew and Greek. His English style was elegant and reverent, homely and clear. In many places it refined carefully and moderately Tyndale's work. More than all else, his love to and reverence of the Scriptures come across clearly. *As for the commendation of God's Holy Scripture, I would fain magnify it, as it is worthy, but I am far insufficient thereto.... Exhorting thee dear reader, so to love it, so to cleave unto it, and so to follow it in thy daily conversation, that other men, seeing thy good works and the fruit of the Holy Ghost in thee, may praise the Father of heaven, and give His Word a good report.* (1535 Prologue)

So where does Coverdale stand in the ranks of those worthies who undertook the uncomfortable and dangerous work in those early years? Professor Mozley, who studied the subject over many years, had this to say: *(Coverdale) was a modest man; he made no great claims for himself, he had no soaring ambitions... he was content that his version should last but a few years and then be superseded by others. But like Tyndale, he built better than he knew... and in the line of scholars who made our King James Bible the name of Coverdale stands second only to Tyndale.* [8]

The 1535 Bible is a combination of Tyndale's flair and genius and Coverdale's consistency and judgment. Space can be given only for a small number of examples.

Coverdale's rendering (in brackets) where different from Tyndale <u>underlined</u>:

Genesis 3.1   But the serpent was subtler than all the beasts of the field which the Lord God had made, and said unto the woman. <u>Ah sir, that God hath said</u> (Yea hath God said in deed), ye shall not eat of all manner of trees in the garden(?). And the woman said unto the serpent, of the fruit of the trees in the garden we may eat, but <u>of</u> (as for) the fruit of the tree that is in the midst of the garden <u>said God</u> (God hath said) <u>see that ye eat not, and see that ye touch it not</u> (eat ye not of it, and touch it not): lest ye die.

Jonah 2.1-2   But the Lord prepared a great fish to swallow up Jonas. <u>And</u> so was Jonas in the <u>bowels</u> (belly) of the fish three days and three nights. And Jonas prayed unto the Lord his God out of the <u>bowels of the fish</u> (fish's belly). And <u>he</u> said: in my <u>tribulation</u> (trouble) I called unto the Lord, and he <u>answered</u> (heard) me: out of the belly of hell I cried and thou heardest my voice.

Hebrews 11.1-2   Faith is a sure confidence of things which are hoped for, and a certainty of things which are not seen. By it the elders were well reported of. Through faith we understand that the world <u>was ordained by the word of God: and that things which are seen, were made of things which are not seen.</u> (and all things which are seen, were made of nought by the word of God).

Coverdale found the greatest difficulty in those parts of the Old Testament where he had fewest guides, and his own lack of Hebrew made him over-dependent on the Latin renderings. One example of a well known text will suffice:

Isaiah 53.1-2.   But who hath given credence unto our preaching? Or to whom is the arm of the Lord known? He shall grow before the Lord like as a branch, as a root in a dry ground.   He shall have neither beauty nor favour.   When we look upon him, there shall be no fairness: we shall have no lust unto him.

Not least of Coverdale's contributions was his understanding that the Hebrew Psalms were in metre to allow for singing as well as reading, and therefore needed to maintain a similar rhythm in translation. Consequently, his Psalms (from the Great Bible) were included for reading and singing in the 1549 Book of Common Prayer and from there into each successive edition down to 1662, which edition has been (decreasingly) used in the Church of England to the present day. It is Coverdale's Psalms which over the intervening four centuries have been the basis of much of the worship of that church.

His own confession is worthy of notice: *It was neither my labour nor desire to have this work put in my hand: nevertheless it grieved me that other nations should be more plenteously provided for with the Scriptures in their mother-tongue, than we: therefore when I was instantly required, though I could not do so well as I would, I thought it yet my duty to do my best, and that with good will. (Prologue to 1535 Bible)*

Perhaps one issue where Coverdale was less sure-footed was in the translation of the Greek words *metanoeo* and *metanoia*. Tyndale not only translated these words as *repent* and *repentance* 54 times out of the 58 times they occur in the New Testament (the other four times he uses *amend* twice, *turn from* and *be converted*), but also in his prologue he gives clear reasons as to why the word *penance* should not be used. Coverdale used *repent* and *repentance* 35 times, *amend* 11 times and *penance* 10 times (*be converted* once and *turn from* once). It is just possible that Coverdale, knowing that King Henry's approval was in the balance and that he might authorise the Bible, wanted to avoid the king's disapproval. He was clearly not entirely comfortable with this matter, as in the prologue he makes clear that his use of the term *penance* was not to suggest any works of man would merit God's favour. It is worthy of note that in the Great Bible, produced only four years later, Coverdale uses *repent* throughout.

Who financed the translation and paid for the printing of the Coverdale Bible? It would seem that it was Jacob van Meteren, merchant of Antwerp. In 1609 his son Emanuel, of the London Dutch church, states that his father was *a furtherer of reformed religion, as he that caused the first Bible at his costs be englished by Mr Myles Coverdale in Antwerp.* [9] Mozley states that in that very year of 1535, Jacob was in trouble. Being away in England perhaps organising the sale of the Bible, his home was visited by officials searching for forbidden books. These lay in a chest which the officers several times laid hands on, but refrained from opening!

Was the 1535 Coverdale Bible printed in Antwerp?

Many articles have been written by historians, arguing on the small matter of where the Coverdale Bible was printed. Zurich, Cologne and Marburg have all been offered as possible locations. An article in the Tyndale Society Journal of November 1997 by Guido Latre seems to have settled this particular question, unless clearer evidence emerges, arguing fairly convincingly for Antwerp on the following grounds:

- The argument that Coverdale had to look elsewhere owing to the danger of printing in Antwerp ignores the fact that large numbers of Dutch Bibles were printing there at that time, an even more dangerous activity, given the hostility to the Reformation of their Spanish rulers. At least the English merchants had a degree of diplomatic immunity.
- Tyndale, Coverdale and Rogers were all living in Antwerp in 1534-5. Everything printed by Tyndale after his return from Hamburg was printed at Antwerp as was Rogers' Bible of 1537.
- Coverdale was employed by one of the foremost printers in Antwerp as a proof-reader and was well known to the printing community there.
- The translation was financed by Antwerp merchant Jacob van Meteren.
- The largest diagram (twice displayed) in Coverdale's Bible is of the tabernacle pitched in the wilderness by Moses. The labels are in the Dutch low German dialect, not in the middle German of Cologne or the Swiss-German of Zurich.
- 80% of Dutch woodcuts at that time were produced in Antwerp.
- Six of the woodcut illustrations used in the Coverdale Bible of 1535 were also used two years later in the Matthews Bible which was printed in Antwerp.

To complicate the matter of printing, Parliament had passed a law in 1534 to protect English book-binders. The law required books to be put together and bound in England. This would explain why James Nicholson, a Fleming, came to London and obtained citizenship in February 1535. Residing at Southwark, he did the importing, buying the printed sheets from van Meteren, binding into book form and selling in England.

Such was the significance of the publication of the first complete printed English Bible that on 4th October 1835, 300 years to the day after the issue of Coverdale's Bible, *sermons and discourses were delivered in nearly all the Protestant churches and chapels throughout the kingdom in commemoration of the Reformation and of the tercentenary of the publication of the first English Bible.* [10]   A medal was struck, and a reprint by Samuel Bagster of the Coverdale Bible issued, the first since 1552.

Bottom part of the title page of the 1535 Bible showing Henry VIII dispensing Bibles.

How was the Bible received by Henry VIII?

The next mountain was the king, and how he would receive the Bible.   As late as December 1534 Tyndale's New Testament was being publicly burned by the Chancellor of England.   Also Bishop Tunstall, typical of most senior churchmen, now removed from London to Durham, was still writing: *Children of iniquity, maintainers of Luther's sect, blinded through extreme wickedness ... craftily have translated the New Testament into our English tongue.* [11] However, much changed in a very short time. The king divorced Catherine of Aragon in 1533 and for three short years his second wife Anne Boleyn was an influence. It would seem that by her intercession, permission was given for the Bible in English to be available, and that *she commanded an English Bible to be laid on the desk in her chamber so that all might read when they would.* [12] In a letter, written many years later, we have evidence of the king's reaction.

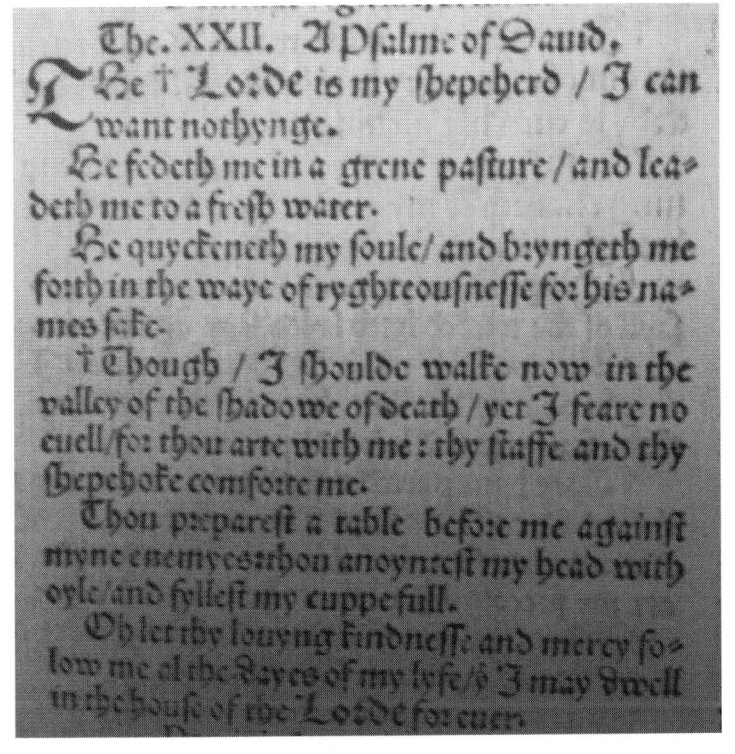

> The. XXII. A Psalme of Dauid.
>
> The Lorde is my shepeherd / I can want nothynge.
>
> He fedeth me in a grene pasture / and leadeth me to a fresh water.
>
> He quyckeneth my soule / and bryngeth me forth in the waye of ryghteousnesse for his names sake.
>
> Though I shoulde walke now in the valley of the shadowe of death / yet I feare no euell / for thou arte with me : thy staffe and thy shepehoke comforte me.
>
> Thou preparest a table before me agaynst myne enemyes : thou anoyntest my head with oyle / and fyllest my cuppe full.
>
> Oh let thy louyng kindnesse and mercy folow me all the dayes of my lyfe / & I may dwell in the house of the Lorde for euer.

Psalm 22 (now 23) from the 1535 Bible (by kind permission of the Trustees of The Devon and Exeter Institution).

I myself, and so did many hundreds beside me hear Dr Coverdale, of holy and learned memory, in a sermon at

Paul's Cross, upon occasion of some slanderous reports that then were raised against his translation, declare his faithful purpose in doing the same: which after it was finished and presented to king Henry VIII, and by him committed to divers bishops of that time to peruse ... and being demanded by the king what was their judgment of the translation, they answered that there were many faults therein. 'Well' said the king, 'but are there any heresies maintained thereby?' They answered that there were no heresies that they could find maintained thereby. 'If there be no heresies' said the king, 'then in God's name let it go abroad among our people. [13]

By early 1536 the Bible was in circulation in London. One further problem beset the 1535 Bible before it came into general use. It was dedicated to the king and *your dearest just wife and most virtuous princess, Queen Anne.* However, tragically within a few weeks of the appearance of the Bible, the *virtuous princess Queen Anne* had been executed by her tyrannical husband and replaced with his third wife, Jane Seymour. The dedication was soon amended and reprinted.

The printing of the English Bible was a milestone in British history. Coverdale's 1535 Bible was reprinted four times, twice in 1537 and then in 1550 and 1552. Its impact was immediate and long-lasting. Daniell makes the point powerfully: *The revolution in religion represented here must not be mistaken. A pre-Reformation mass was conducted at the distant altar by the priest murmuring in Latin with his back to the people. In a post-Reformation service, the minister faced his congregation and addressed them in English.... Everyone used a service book made of copious quotations from the Bible in English.* [14] It was a movement in the opposite direction to that which had occurred one thousand years before. Speaking of the leaving off of translating the Scriptures into other tongues after the times of Augustine, Coverdale says: *As soon as the Bible was cast aside, and no more put into exercise, then began everyone of his own head to write whatsoever came into his brain, and that seemed good in his own eyes; and so grew the darkness of men's traditions.* (Prologue to 1535 Bible) No longer!

As an interesting footnote, 65 copies of the 1535 Coverdale Bible were identified in 1974 in the English speaking world, including 26 copies in the USA and 38 in UK. Twelve others are known to exist [15] There are perhaps a few more undiscovered and in non-English-speaking countries. A copy from Dr Charles Ryrie's library was auctioned in New York in 2016 for US$ 348,500.

Coverdale was now to return to England; to a very different England from the one he had left seven years before. The king's great matter, his divorce, had changed the climate in which the early Reformers were at work.

Chapter 5

Working for Thomas Cromwell

Who hath holden the wind fast in his hand?. Who hath comprehended all the waters in a garment? Who hath set all the ends of the world? What is his name, or his Son's name? Canst thou tell? All the words of God are pure and clean, for He is a shield unto all them that put their trust in him. Put thou nothing therefore unto His words, lest he reprove thee and thou be found as a liar. (Proverbs 30 block A)

Political changes in England 1529-35

So what had changed in England? The answer is that the whole framework of laws and authority had been turned upside down. In 1529, when Coverdale left for his first exile, the Reformers were being hounded, imprisoned, fined and even burned at the stake for owning and reading their English New Testaments, or preaching contrary to the authority of the Roman Catholic Church in England. In 1535, Thomas Cromwell, Thomas Cranmer and Anne Boleyn, three who favoured the Reformation, were influential around the king. Cardinal Wolsey, the king's first minister, Bishop Fisher and Sir Thomas More had all been or were about to be destroyed by the arbitrary power of Henry VIII. The king had replaced the Pope with his own rule as Head of the Church of England. How did it happen?

By 1529, Catherine of Aragon, the king's first wife was 45 years old. She had one daughter, Princess Mary, and was probably beyond childbearing age. Only once, briefly, had

England ever been ruled by a woman - Matilda. This was not a success. The king was desperate for a male heir and wanted grounds for a divorce so that the Tudor line could continue. He thought he found grounds in the Bible (Leviticus chapters 18 and 20), forbidding marriage with a deceased brother's wife. Catherine had briefly been married to Henry's older brother who died young. Wolsey assured the king that the Pope would have no trouble granting an annulment, and in normal circumstances this would have been correct. However, Pope Clement VII was in the power of Catherine's nephew, Charles V. His soldiers, perhaps out of control at the time, had sacked Rome in 1527. Charles V was not prepared to see his aunt abandoned and the family honour insulted. Three years after Wolsey had begun to move the king's great matter forward and, owing to his lack of success, Henry lost patience and in 1529 Wolsey fell from power.

This marked the beginning of the rise of Thomas Cromwell. More, Wolsey's replacement as Lord Chancellor, in the Council, and John Fisher, Bishop of Rochester, were able to keep the reins of power for a short time longer to 1532. But Thomas Cromwell, with the king's favour, began to use the House of Commons to air grievances against the Church. Parliament was of some importance, even before the days of Henry VIII. He could not impose taxes without their consent. The limits of Parliament's powers were ill-defined and sometimes kings stepped outside those limits. However, as Macaulay put it: *In the monarchies of the Middle Ages the power of the sword belonged to the prince, but the power of the purse belonged to the nation; and the progress of civilisation, as it made the sword of the prince more and more formidable to the nation, made the purse of the nation more and more necessary to the prince.* [1] When the House of Commons met in 1529, it soon began to list the grievances of the nation against the clergy – the exacting of great sums from the people for the enrichment of the clergy, taxing the people without their agreement, the cruel treatment meted out for heresy, and the giving of livings to infants and children, whereby the priests left the people without teaching. One example, the sixth head of the grievance sent by the Commons to the King was: *one priest being little learned, had ten or twelve benefices, and was resident in none, and many well-learned scholars in the university, who were able to preach and teach had neither benefice nor exhibition.* Henry, at the request of the Commons, sent the list to the bishops and demanded a reply. Led by Fisher, a bold and learned Renaissance scholar determined to defend the Roman Catholic church, their reply was uncompromising. Who were these laymen? And to complain that the clergy were suppressing heresy; was that not part of the role of the clergy? Other measures followed through the House of Commons; one to prevent priests from holding large estates, or carrying on big business. A further law banned plurality of benefices, another non-residence of clergy. When Parliament rose in December 1529, it had taken the first steps reducing the power of the Church over the lives of the ordinary people.

After some further measures to put pressure on the Pope, in February 1533 Thomas Cromwell came up with a simple solution to the problem of Papal veto on the divorce. Could the powers exercised in Rome be returned to London? On behalf of the king, he brought to the House of Commons what was to become the Act in Restraint of Appeals, making it illegal for any English subject to appeal to an ecclesiastical court outside England. This passed into law a power given to the King over matters spiritual, including the appointment of bishops, as well as matters temporal. The Pope's reply was to excommunicate Henry.

The king had little difficulty seeing his way forward! On 9th June 1534 Henry signed a proclamation: *That having been acknowledged next after God, supreme head of the Church of England, he abolished the authority of the bishop of Rome throughout his realm, and commanded all bishops to preach every Sunday and Holy Day the true and sincere Word of the Lord; to teach that the jurisdiction of the Church belongs to him alone, and to blot out of all canons, liturgies and other works the name of the bishop of Rome and his pompous titles, so that his name and memory be never more remembered in the kingdom of England.* [2]

A further motive for the sweeping changes was the King's continuing need for money to support his lavish lifestyle. It is estimated that the annual income of the state at that time was £100,000, and that of the monasteries 60% greater. [3] It took little persuasion from Thomas Cromwell for the king to replenish his exhausted treasury by laying hands on these golden eggs once the Church of England came under his authority. By the time of Coverdale's return in 1535 Thomas Cromwell, who was the architect of much of this change, was at the peak of his power as the King's first minister, the first to exercise authority through the House of Commons. He was also *Vice-Gerant in Spirituals*, an office not known before or since. It allowed him to exercise authority over the Church of England on the king's behalf.

Another friend to the Reformation was Cambridge scholar Thomas Cranmer. Cranmer's advice to the king, which he wrote out at Henry's command, was that it was not agreeable to Scripture to marry one's brother's wife, and the bishop of Rome had no authority to dispense with the Scriptures. Now Henry, in his anxiety to find a solution to his quest to be free from his first wife, began to look more favourably at the teaching of the Reformers. Cranmer's reward for his help was to be appointed Archbishop of Canterbury on 30th March 1533. He was at the king's elbow gently moving the Church of England a step at a time in a Reformed direction. This he continued to do until the death of Edward VI twenty years later.

A third friend of the Reformers was Anne Boleyn. In July 1531, the king required Catherine of Aragon to retire from court. He never saw her again. Henry then went through the formal and legal steps to divorce his first wife. The second wife, Queen Anne Boleyn, owed her place to these events. While she may not have had the piety of a true

Portrait of Henry VIII

Reformer, she certainly used her influence in favour of the Reformation. Anne Boleyn, at the end of 1532 or beginning of 1533 was with child. On 23rd May 1533, Cranmer declared the king's first marriage to be void, and on 28th May his marriage to Anne (which had taken place quietly in January) was declared lawful. While the king was infatuated with Anne Boleyn, *her place in the revolution was none other than prospective mother to the heir to the throne.* [4] The daughter born on 7th September 1533, in the midst of this turmoil and confusion was the future Elizabeth I who was to reign in her own right for 44 years.

There is evidence that under the influence of Anne Boleyn, the 1535 Coverdale Bible might well have been authorised by Henry VIII. The draft injunction, produced by Cromwell in 1536, originally contained a command for the Bible to be set up and read in every church. However, in May of that year came Anne Boleyn's fall from the unpredictable king's favour, her arrest and execution. Cromwell clearly felt this was not the time to push an issue closely connected with the fallen queen.

Although Henry split with Rome over his divorce, it was to liberate himself not his people. So while on the one hand the king saw the usefulness of the Reformed party in his dispute with the Pope, he had little sympathy with their doctrines. Rule by Rome and the priests was to be replaced by rule by the king, who took the place of the Pope as Head of the Church. The extent to which the cause of the Reformation prospered in official circles depended on which party had the king's ear. On the side of reform were Cranmer, Latimer (at this point elevated to be Bishop of Worcester), Thomas Cromwell and Anne Boleyn. They were much hampered by enemies ready to try to pull them down and poison the king against them – successfully in the case of the last two. On the side favouring the Roman Catholic Church were those who refused to transfer their allegiance from Pope to King. To support their influence, the Pope decided to give Bishop Fisher a cardinal's hat. With grim 'humour', Henry growled that by the time it reached England, Fisher would not have a head to put it on. He and Sir Thomas More were executed in 1535, both men dying bravely as committed Roman Catholics, refusing to change their allegiance at the king's orders or to take the oath of submission to Henry as Head of the Church in England. A number of Carthusian priors also, who had refused to take the oath, found their monasteries taken away and were executed for the same reason. The king would brook no opposition. Fourteen Anabaptists were burned at this time, too, as Henry asserted his absolute power in every direction.

The papal party in England seemed to be failing on every count in 1533-35. The blows had fallen quickly – the divorce, a new queen, the loss of the supremacy of the Pope, and the executions of Fisher and More. However, the ceremonials, the Latin rites and the teaching of the Church of England changed but little during the remainder of Henry's reign, except where Reformers were able to influence him. But the tide had turned during Coverdale's seven years in exile sufficiently for him to return without having to compromise his beliefs.

Coverdale's activities back in England

Coverdale supported and helped Thomas Cromwell wherever he could in pushing forward the Reformation. Our first glimpse of him is from a certain John Prowse reporting to Coverdale by letter. Clearly they were working for Thomas Cromwell who had sent Prowse with letters to the mayors of Winchelsea and Rye. On receipt of the letters the mayor of Winchelsea had immediately committed the Prior of the local monastery to prison. *He is a very unthift priest and a great reveller.* Clearly the prompt action had a sobering effect on the citizens. *The people of Rye were daily likely to riot until their parson was in prison. Now all was quiet!* [5] That Prowse was reporting to Coverdale suggests that already he was playing an active role in visiting monasteries, reporting on abuses and reforming the Church.

During his first three years back in England Coverdale, too, was at his ongoing work of translating various writings from German into English. To give an idea of his industry and how forward he was to ensure his countrymen had access to the best Reformation works available from Europe, in the year 1537 alone he produced, and printer James Nicholson sold, ten works: two new editions of his 1535 Bible, two of the New Testament, one of the Books of Solomon, and five translations from German teachers. His productions included English translations of Luther's commentary on the Magnificat (Mary's Song of worship in Gospel of Luke 1. 46-55), and of the 23rd Psalm (called Psalm 22 in the early Bibles).

One further service to the cause of religion in England which Coverdale was well placed to achieve was to make accessible in English some of the popular Psalms and hymns which Luther and others had composed for Germany. Having lived among Lutherans during his exile, he had seen at first hand the effect of Luther's hymns.

Martin Luther ... may be called the originator of hymns, as we now understand the word. Gifted as he was, with a peculiar talent for music, he brought this at once into the service of the sanctuary; and possessing a style of writing so vigorous and bold, so animated and expressive ... he carried this force and fire with all his native beauty of musical expression into the hymns which flowed from his fertile pen.[6]

D'Aubigne gives the example of a hymn Luther composed about the death of the three Austin Friars burned alive by the Inquisition in the market-place at Brussels in 1523. This hymn, full of energy, was soon widely sung in Germany and the Low Countries. Coverdale published a short selection of Luther's hymns and Psalms which he had translated into English, entitled: *Ghostly Psalms and Spiritual Songs.* This was a new tradition, a first Reformation attempt to introduce Psalm and hymn singing into English, and contained 23 hymns, 15 Psalms and three songs, with simple tunes attached. His motive was to encourage both personal and social singing.

Coverdale writes in the preface to this book: *O that men's lips were so opened, that their mouths might show the praise of God. Yea would God our minstrels, had none other thing to play upon, neither our carters and ploughmen other thing to whistle upon, save psalms, hymns and such godly songs* as David is occupied withal. And if women, spinning at their wheels, had none other songs to pass their time with, than such as Moses' sister and Mary the mother of Christ have sung before them, they should be better occupied than with hey nony nony, hey troly loly, and such like fantasies.[7]

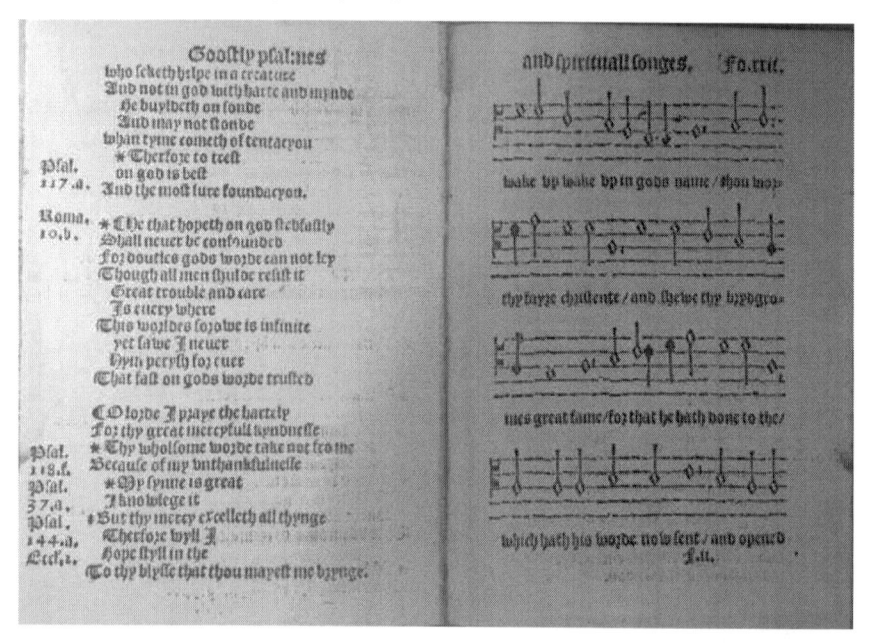

Page from Ghostly Psalms: Used with permission of The Provost and Fellows of The Queen's College, Oxford

Coverdale's introduction to his *Ghostly Psalms and Spiritual Songs* makes clear his motive for this work: *For doubtless, whoso believeth that God loveth him, and feeleth by his faith, that he hath forgiven him all his sins, and careth for him, and delivereth him from all evil; whosoever he be ... shall be compelled by the Spirit of God to break out into praise therefore.* [8]

Coverdale also published a concordance, to help ordinary folk find their way around the 1535 English Bible. This did not have the detail we have come to expect in concordances chiefly because, while this Bible was divided into chapters, as yet there were no verses, each average length chapter being divided into four blocks labelled a-d. Verses came first into English Bibles with the 1560 Geneva Bible.

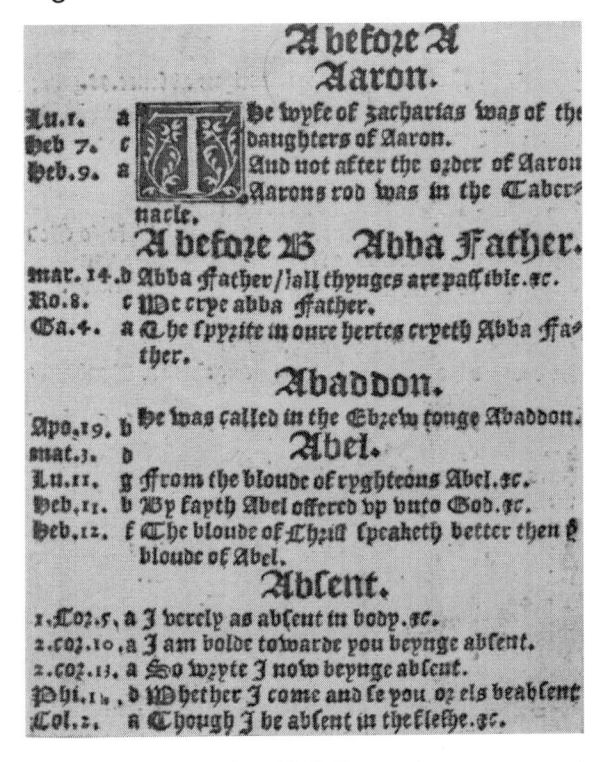

Coverdale's 1535 Concordance
by permission of the Chapter of St Paul's Cathedral

It was at this point of the Reformation in Henry VIII's reign that the Matthews Bible was published in Antwerp. It was the work of John Rogers, the first to be burned at the stake in the reign of Mary. It is thought that when Tyndale was captured Rogers had his papers, including the manuscript of those parts of the Old Testament (Judges to 2 Chronicles) which Tyndale had finished working on when imprisoned. The remainder of the Bible was a light revision from Coverdale's 1535 Bible of those parts which came from Tyndale's work, and a more substantial revision of the remainder of the Old Testament.

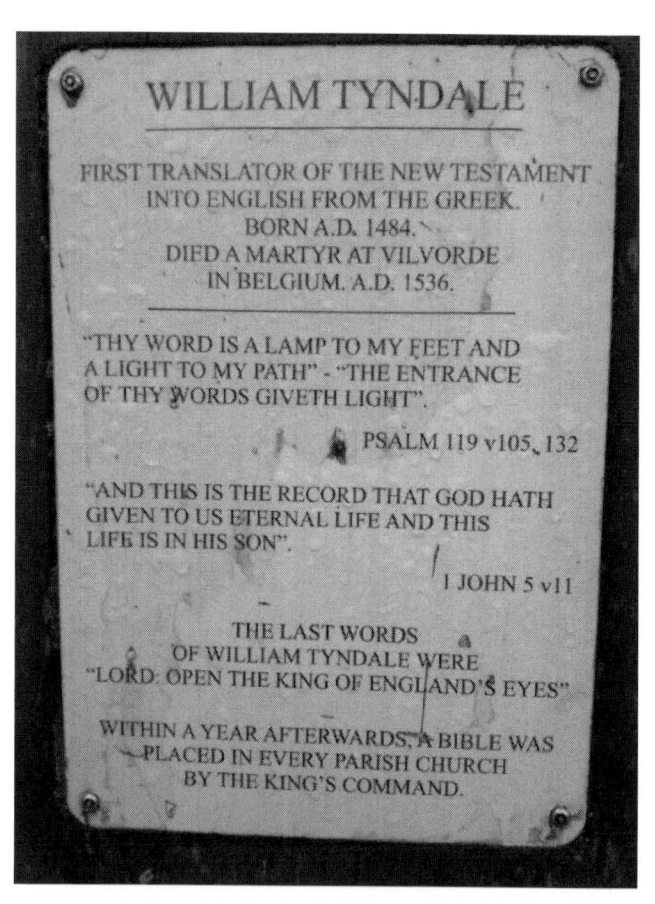

> # WILLIAM TYNDALE
>
> FIRST TRANSLATOR OF THE NEW TESTAMENT
> INTO ENGLISH FROM THE GREEK.
> BORN A.D. 1484.
> DIED A MARTYR AT VILVORDE
> IN BELGIUM. A.D. 1536.
>
> "THY WORD IS A LAMP TO MY FEET AND
> A LIGHT TO MY PATH" - "THE ENTRANCE
> OF THY WORDS GIVETH LIGHT".
>
> PSALM 119 v105, 132
>
> "AND THIS IS THE RECORD THAT GOD HATH
> GIVEN TO US ETERNAL LIFE AND THIS
> LIFE IS IN HIS SON".
>
> I JOHN 5 v11
>
> THE LAST WORDS
> OF WILLIAM TYNDALE WERE
> "LORD: OPEN THE KING OF ENGLAND'S EYES"
>
> WITHIN A YEAR AFTERWARDS, A BIBLE WAS
> PLACED IN EVERY PARISH CHURCH
> BY THE KING'S COMMAND.

Memorial to Tyndale on the Embankment in London. The last sentence is not quite accurate, as many churches did not buy a copy of the Bible until after Cromwell's later injunction of 1539, and the production of the Great Bible.

Rogers was an excellent scholar, with a good working knowledge of Hebrew and Greek. To his translation he added over 2000 notes of explanation and clarification, some of which were clearly anti-Papal. (Coverdale felt unwilling to add notes to his 1535 Bible, and at Cromwell's advice refrained from doing so in the 1539 Great Bible). There was a further addition to the Matthews Bible which infuriated the conservative party in England: a table collecting in one place those texts of Scripture which teach the Lord's Supper as being a service of remembrance and also supporting the marriage of priests. At that point they could do nothing about it, other than to bide their time.

When Cranmer received a copy of this Bible on 4th August 1537, he sent it to Thomas Cromwell, asking him to request the king to licence it, which the king, in an expansive mood as Jane Seymour (his third wife) neared the end of her pregnancy, was pleased to do. Cromwell, taking his cue from this, allowed Nicholson to reprint the Coverdale Bible before the end of 1537, also having on the title page: *Set forth with the king's most gracious licence.* It is worthy of note that when Tyndale died at the stake, his last reported prayer was: *Lord open the King of England's eyes.* Just over a year later, both of the English printed Bibles in circulation went out under the king's licence.

Coverdale's Great Bible

Cromwell now spurred on the bishops. His first injunction of 1538 specified that in all the churches, *the Bible, both in Latin and also in English should lie in the choir for every man that will to read therein.* He was warmly supported by the evangelical bishops such as Cranmer and Latimer. To supply some of the lack, Coverdale provided a Latin and English New Testament in 1538, before setting off for France. This book was to contain the Vulgate Latin edition and a lightly revised English edition of his own, with a short preface which he wrote and left for the printer to prepare and issue. It was published by the printer, entitled *The New Testament both in Latin and English, each corresponding to the other, after the vulgate text commonly called Jerome's. Faithfully translated by Myles Coverdale 1538. Set forth with the King's most gracious licence.* From Coverdale's dedication to Henry VIII we get a tiny glimpse of the determined opposition faced by the early Reformers at this time. *Their inward malice doth break out into blasphemous and uncomely words; insomuch that they call your loving and faithful people heretics, new-fangled fellows, English biblers, coblers of divinity with other such ungodly sayings.*[9]

However, all was not well with this work, and when Coverdale saw a copy of his English-Latin New Testament that summer in Paris, he was much troubled, sufficiently to work on a second edition without delay. The second edition was printed in Paris. A copy was sent to Thomas Cromwell by Grafton the printer. *When Master Coverdale considered and found it so foolishly done, yea and so corrupt, it not only grieved him that the printer had defamed him and his learning by adding his name to so fond a thing, but also that the common people were deprived of the true sense of God's word. Although I have enough to do, I have printed the same again, translated and corrected by Mr Coverdale himself.* [10] No doubt such a distraction would have been less than welcome in the midst of other difficulties Coverdale and the printers were now experiencing in Paris.

On 12th October 1537 Jane Seymour gave birth to the long-awaited son and heir, the future Edward VI. Twelve days later she died. Henry was bereft.

Matters in the Church, however, progressed and in September 1538, Cromwell decided to raise his expectations of the clergy in promoting the Reformation. So, he issued his injunction for a new edition of the Bible. The injunction was: *That ye shall provide one book of the whole Bible of the largest volume in English, and the same set up in some convenient place whereat your parishioners may resort to the same and read it; the charges of which book shall be borne between you the parson and the parishioners, that is to say, one half by you and the other half of them.* Hence the 14" x 9" Great Bible.

A glimpse of the poverty of the land and the foresight of Cromwell can be seen in a 1540 letter from a rector in Kent to one of Cromwell's servants, asking for financial help to place a copy of the Great Bible in the parish church. *We have but one that can read it, and but sixteen householders, and not four good ploughs of them all and not able to pay 5s amongst them all, and my portion is so small (as rector) that I am not able to pay more.* [11] We are not told Cromwell's response but the provision of one Bible for community use (the cost was 10 shillings unbound and 12 shillings bound: a considerable sum for those times) was a powerful stimulus to literacy as well as the work of the Reformation. (The currency convertor at the National Archives states that £1 in 1540 is equal to £420 today.)

Who was to supervise the work? Cromwell's selection of Coverdale was no doubt partly due to the friendship between the two men. Coverdale had a greater and wider experience of translation work than any other, and his amiable and modest character would avoid needless offence in an often hostile political environment, without compromising essential principles. Coverdale himself, no doubt feeling that his friend John Rogers had improved and refined his own 1535 Bible, chose to base his work on the Matthews Bible of 1537 (which itself owed a great debt to his own earlier work). It is described by historian A G Dickens as follows: *The success of the Great Bible proved no more than its just desert, for it turned out to be Coverdale's masterpiece.... a sober, tasteful, workmanlike production.* [11a] The publishing was to be done by Grafton and Whitchurch who had produced the Matthews Bible. As the costs increased, Cromwell himself contributed £400 to the project.

The best quality printing was being done in Paris at this time, so there Coverdale went to pursue his work. Cromwell sent a letter from Henry VIII to the King of France, asking him *to permit and licence a subject of his to imprint the Bible in English within the University of Paris, which licence was granted so long as the book contained 'no private or unlawful opinions'.*

However, on 23rd June 1538, Coverdale was writing to Cromwell to report not only that the work was going forward, but also the hostility with which they were surrounded. *We be entered into your work of the Bible, whereof we have here sent unto your lordship two ensamples; one in parchment, wherein we intend to print one for the king's grace, and another for your lordship;* (these two copies still exist) *and the second in paper, whereof all the rest shall be made.... We (if need require) in our just business to be defended from the papists by your lordship's favourable letters, which we most humbly desire to have.... We be daily threatened.* [12]

Woodcut of Joseph being put in the pit by his brethren: Great Bible

Further reports from Coverdale to Cromwell were sent on 9th August explaining how far they had progressed and their motives: *As God Almighty moved your lordship to set us unto it, so shall it be to His glory, and right welcome to all them that love to serve Him and their prince in true faithful obedience.* [12]

The storm clouds, however, were gathering quickly. On 13th December Coverdale wrote to Cromwell asking whether he should add notes of explanation to the Great Bible. More ominously, he flagged up to Cromwell that the project was now in danger in Paris. *And whereas my said lord of Hereford* (Bishop Edmund Bonner) *is so good unto us to convey thus much of the bible to your good lordship, I humbly beseech the same to be defender and keeper thereof, to the intent that if these men proceed in their cruelness against us, and confiscate the rest, yet this at the least may be safe by the means of your lordship.* Four days later, the threatened calamity fell on them. [12a] Their host Regnault was cited before the Inquisition, with other persons unnamed who were engaged in printing an English Bible. Foxe tells us that the Inquisitors sent for the Englishmen *that were at the cost and charge thereof, and also such as had the correction of the same which was Myles Coverdale, but having some warning what would follow, the said Englishmen posted away as fast as they could to save themselves, leaving behind them all their Bibles, which were to the number 2,500.* [13]

So what stopped the printing in France? There is little doubt that a large number of enemies of this project were on hand. On 24th December 1538 the Pope gave instruction that *the bible corruptly translated into English may either not be published or burnt.* [14] There were also plenty of opponents in both France and England only too ready to put pressure on the French authorities to stop the work.

Foxe tells us that after the project transferred to London, it was *not without great trouble and loss, for the hatred of the bishops, namely Stephen Gardiner, and his fellows, who mightily did stomach and malign the printing thereof.* In France the church party was even stronger and the friends of the Reformation weaker, so that however much Francis I might wish to be friendly to Henry VIII, the opposing forces were too strong for him.

However, with judicious pressure applied by Cromwell through the seizure on a French ship for piracy, which the French government wanted back, the type, printers and paper were sent over to England and the printing completed

Woodcut from the Great Bible of the building of the Tower of Babel

in London in April 1539. Six further editions were printed in 1540-1, and to the second edition Cranmer added a famous preface, so that the Great Bible is often and inaccurately called *Cranmer's Bible.* Coverdale made some revisions to the second and third editions, but after that he was in exile. Some ten further editions of the Great Bible were printed in the reigns of Edward VI and Elizabeth I, ending in 1568 when the replacement Bishops Bible became the official edition favoured by the Crown. The Great Bible is the first in English to follow the same order of the sixty-six books which make up the King James Bible.

It would seem that Bible-reading by ordinary folk was now becoming more common-place. *It was wonderful,* says Strype, *to see with what joy this Book of God was received, not only among the learneder sort, but among all the vulgar and common people; and with what greediness God's Word was read, and what resort to places where the reading of it was.* [14a]

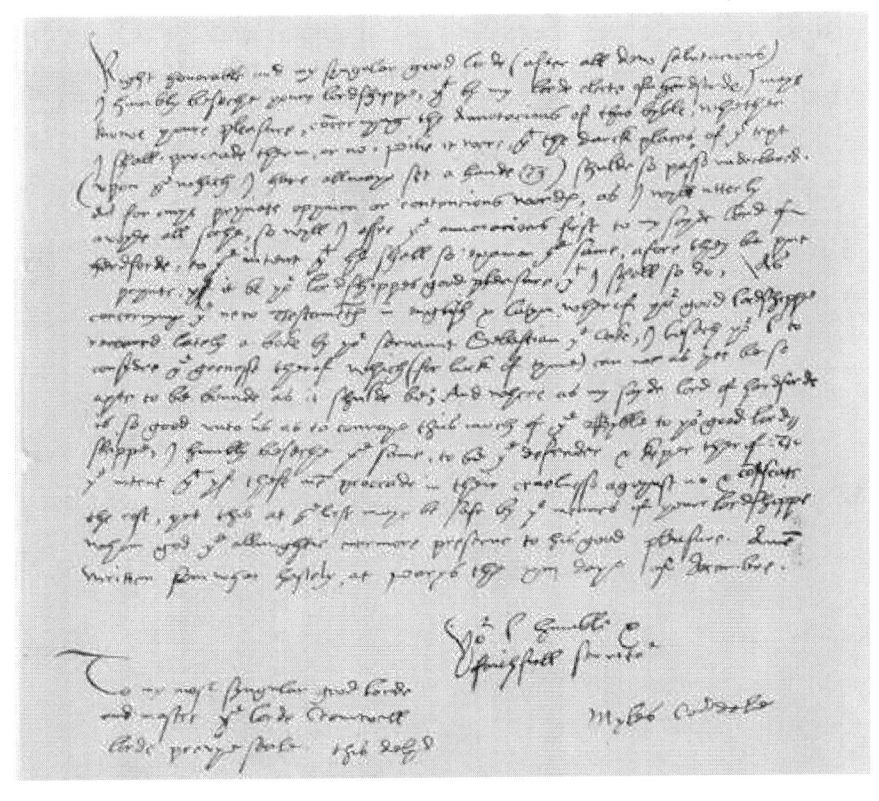

Copy of a letter from Coverdale to Thomas Cromwell 13th December 1538. A copy is in the British Library (Add. MS 26670)

Coverdale at Newbury; his marriage

After returning to England in 1539, and with his part in the Great Bible completed, Coverdale was given other work to do. Because the Church of England was now established by law it was enforced by injunctions issued by Thomas Cromwell in the name of the King. Bibles were to be placed in every church, the Lord's Prayer and the Ten Commandments to be taught line-by-line on Sundays, and at least one sermon was to be preached every three months. Coverdale, it would seem, was sent by Cromwell as a visitor to Newbury in the diocese of Salisbury to discover how much progress was being made. His report was not very encouraging; further evidence of the comparatively small numbers favouring the Reformation at this time. He wrote to Cromwell on 8th February 1539 and again on 5th March: *This is to advertise the same, that for lack of diligent inquisition, and through overmuch sufferance, there are in these countries (and so I fear me in many more) an innumerable sort of such popish books, as not only be incorrect, but are also great occasion to keep the king's subjects still in error ... wheresoever I understand any such unlawful books to be, I may correct them, or cause them to be corrected. In the executing whereof I do not doubt but to win the parties, and to make them not only more fervent toward God and his word, but also to increase in due obedience toward the king's highness.* [15]

Newbury Parish Church in which Coverdale preached.

As Coverdale knew, however, the traditions of the Church from earlier years still had a strong hold on the people, especially when there was no interest in reform at the top. As he complains to Cromwell in a further letter: *A great number of the priests of this realm ... have not utterly extinct all such ecclesiastical service, as is against his grace's most lawful supremacy and prerogative. For in the feast called Cathedra S. Petri a great part of their matins is plainly a maintenance of the B. of Rome's usurped power. This is evident in all the great matin-books of the church of Newbury, and I doubt not but it is so likewise in many churches more.* [16]

Moving on to nearby Henley, administered as part of the diocese of Lincoln, with a bishop more hostile to the Reformation, evidence appears of a deeper level of tradition and superstitious practice in the churches, supposedly newly reformed: *In a glass window of our lady chapel in the church of the said Henley the image of Thomas a Becket, with the whole feigned story of his death, is suffered to stand still. Not only this, but that all the beams, irons, and candlesticks, whereupon tapers and lights were wont to be set up unto images, remain still untaken down; whereby the poor simple unlearned people believe that they shall have liberty to set up their candles again unto images, and that the old fashion shall shortly return ... I reckon great and notable negligence in the bishop of Lincoln, which, being so nigh thereby, doth not weed out such faults; yea, I fear it be as evil, or worse, in many more places of his diocese.* [17]

It would seem that while in the diocese of Salisbury, Coverdale met and married Elizabeth Macheson. It is likely that she was living in the Cathedral Close in Salisbury at this time, with her sister Agnes, and brother-in-law John Macalpine. Macalpine's name appears in the Cathedral archives as resident there for some seven months from July 1538 to the Spring of 1539, after coming south from Scotland. [18] Like Coverdale, he soon went into exile once marriage of priests was made illegal in the summer of 1539. This suggests that Coverdale probably married in the early part of 1539. He would hardly have taken a wife after that time as the penalty for married clergymen under the Act of Six Articles 1539 was clearly set out. *All marriages of priests are declared void, and if any priest did still keep any woman whom he had so married, he shall suffer death by hanging as a felon, the woman to suffer in the same manner as the priests.*

In the short but precious window of time left before persecution closed in again, Coverdale found time for two more publications in 1539. The king had appointed a clerical commission to draw up those matters essential for a Christian man to observe. The result, known as the King's Book, was published in due course and was a battleground between the Reformers, led by Cranmer and the traditionalists, led by Gardiner, with the king weighing in from time to time. Coverdale drew up a *General Confession* which was designed to influence the work of this group but, because he felt it would be profitable to a wider public, he published it. No doubt there was a hope that it would reinforce arguments made by the Reformed group on the clerical commission, and encourage them not to water down their input in the face of pressure from the other side. Coverdale appeared before the Privy Council to present his General Confession in 1539, no doubt at the invitation of either Cranmer or Cromwell. [19] It was Coverdale's hope that it might be used in the Communion Service of the Church of England. However, the high water mark had now passed for a few years, not to return until the death of the old king.

Coverdale's other publication, a Catechism upon the Creed, was designed to help ministers carry out Cromwell's Injunctions. The idea was to take one clause at a time of the Apostle's Creed, which parish priests were to teach, offering Bible texts and comments to support it. This was not dissimilar to the work produced in his second exile, *Fruitful Works*, in which Coverdale mentioned this 1539 publication.

However, much was about to change in England. The king was now swinging back to favour the traditionalist party. In the king's opinion, his half-way Reformation had gone far enough. Coverdale went into exile again, after five short years working for Thomas Cromwell.

Chapter 6

Second exile.   Suffering reproach

When they persecute you in one city, fly in to another.   I tell you for a truth, ye shall not finish all the cities of Israel, till the son of man come.   The disciple is not above the master, neither the servant above the Lord.   It is enough for the disciple to be as his master, and the servant as his Lord.   If they have called the good man of the house Beelzebub, how much more shall they call them of his household so?   Fear them not therefore. (Matthew 10 Block C)

Why did Coverdale leave England?

To all intents the publication of the Great Bible in April 1539, authorised by the king and commissioned by First Minister Thomas Cromwell should have been a stepping stone to high office in the Church or one of the universities for Coverdale, as a reward from a grateful king and nation. But in 1540 Coverdale went into exile again, this time for eight years, until the death of Henry VIII.   What had gone wrong?

To understand, we must return to 1536.   The Reformation had not progressed very far, as shown by Coverdale's letters from Newbury.   A small number of Reformed preachers were at work, helped on by Cranmer and Cromwell who, as able, persuaded the king to make changes in the Church of England.   1536 produced an important document from the Church of England: the Ten

Articles. It was a mixture of old and new. Above all, it reflected the king's conservatism and his inner distaste for the new teaching. The Ten Articles, which were to be followed in the churches, cast doubts on purgatory, reduced the seven Roman Catholic sacraments to three and included such terms as justification and faith. However, they also taught image worship and the 'real presence' in the Lord's Supper.

It was at this point that the most serious popular rebellion of Henry's reign blew up, the 'Pilgrimage of Grace'. The rebellion began in Lincolnshire in September 1536, and then spread to Yorkshire. Three sets of government commissioners were at work, one dissolving the smaller monasteries, the second collecting taxes and the third enforcing the Ten Articles on the clergy and parishes. In this atmosphere, the clergy whipped up their hearers in open rebellion and 10,000 marched on Lincoln demanding a halt to the Reformation and to the dissolutions. On the arrival of the Duke of Suffolk with a royal army, the rebels were appeased and persuaded to return home. However, by October and November, the rising had spread to Yorkshire and the northern counties and assumed a more threatening form. A number of the nobles and gentry joined the rebellion, which took control of certain towns east of the Pennines in Yorkshire, Durham and Northumberland. Henry rejected their demands, but promised they would be debated in Parliament and the rebels given a general pardon. Henry had no intention to keep faith and when a third rebellion grew out of the second, in January 1537 among some who doubted his word, he acted savagely to put it down. For a while, though, things looked threatening. Henry, alert to public opinion, was not going to risk his kingdom for a thorough Reformation he did not believe in.

With the death of Jane Seymour the king, perhaps grieving for her, perhaps because her death made him begin again to contemplate theology, perhaps wishing to put a brake on the rate of change, began to take a more personal interest in the Bishops Book. The Book had begun in 1537 as the higher clergy were called together by Thomas Cromwell to give a clear statement of the beliefs of the Church of England. Cranmer's first draft had a distinctively Lutheran flavour, but at the end of 1537 when the king personally took an interest, he made over 200 amendments to the draft. A central issue between the king and the conservative bishops on one side and Cranmer on the other was their contrasting ideas on salvation. On Cranmer's side was the Biblical picture of fallen humanity, helpless and hopeless because of Adam's disobedience, until the gift of grace through faith was given. On the king's side, supported by most of the bishops, was the view that the human will was able, by the performance of good works and by penance, to earn salvation.

On the back of this rift came the truce between France and Spain, something the king had always feared, as uniting the two most powerful European monarchs of the day. What was to stop them reclaiming England for the Pope? Much of Henry's foreign policy had been aimed at keeping these powers apart. Now his foreign policy became more favourable to Spain as he hoped to win some goodwill from Charles V. This was especially so as he knew the French were casting greedy eyes on Calais. To achieve this goodwill Henry needed to show himself a good Catholic, although minus the Pope! At Easter 1539 the king began by creeping to the cross and attending mass.

The simmering tensions between the two parties in England broke out in 1539. This was the year the Act of Six Articles was passed through Parliament against the opposition of Cranmer. In 1538, Stephen Gardiner, Bishop of Winchester, returned from an embassy to Charles V. Dismayed by what he saw as the lurch of England towards the Reformation, Gardiner soon saw that influencing the king was the key to reversing matters. Henry's revolution was 'Catholicism without the Pope', so there was no use in speaking to him of Papal displeasure. However, the king did not want to see the Emperor and the French king unite against him. Could he show them he was really a loyal son of the Church? After all, he still remained loyal to Church traditions and was opposed to justification by faith – the watchword of the Reformation. These were the arguments used by Gardiner to strike a major blow at the Reformation in 1539. The King, who legalised the English Bible in 1536, and allowed Cromwell to extend its reach in 1538, was the same King who insisted on the Act of Six Articles the 'whip with six strings' in 1539. It did not help the cause of the Reformers that Thomas Cromwell was laid low with illness for much of early 1539 and could not therefore counterbalance the influence of Gardiner.

The Act of Six Articles stated six points of medieval doctrine and practice which the Reformers had begun to assail, and imposed severe penalties on all who would not accept them. They were that:

1   The doctrine of transubstantiation was to be believed.
2   Lay people should not take the wine at the Lord's Supper
3   Priests must not marry
4   Among priests and nuns, the vows of chastity were to be observed
5   Private masses were lawful
6   Confession to a priest was a necessary and important religious duty.

The King required conformity to his religion. The Six Articles were drawn up by the Anglo-Catholic party, now headed by Gardiner, and approved by the king. Cranmer resisted stoutly and alone in the House of Lords for three days, bringing forward many reasons from Scripture against them. No other bishop stood with him. The rest, either from fear of the king stayed away, or from a wish to suppress reformed teaching took the other side. Latimer resigned his bishopric and when the Act came into force in 1540, some 500 Protestants were soon in prison for refusing to conform.

Many others, Coverdale among them, left the country for exile. This Act continued in force for the rest of Henry's reign. Punishment for denying the first Article was to be burned at the stake and for the others, fines on the first occurrence followed by execution for any further offence.

The year 1540 saw an even more marked swing away from the Reformation. This was the year of two queens and the execution of first minister Thomas Cromwell. What really brought Cromwell to the end of his extraordinary career was his attempt to find a fourth wife for Henry, after the death of Jane Seymour in 1537. What better way to strengthen the Reformation than to ally the king with one of the Lutheran princes of northern Germany? The choice fell on Anne of Cleves, sister of the Duke of that state and sister-in-law to the Elector of Saxony. When she arrived in England in January 1540, the king felt repelled by her. As the contracts were signed, he went through with the marriage, but within days was looking for a way out. His wrath fell upon Cromwell, who had been largely responsible for the alliance. In June Cromwell was arrested, taken to the Tower like so many of his victims, and shortly executed

Thomas Cromwell – the King's First Minister and Vice-Gerant (i.e. his deputy) in spiritual matters.

without trial. Foxe wrote: *This is most certain, that the king did afterwards greatly and earnestly repent his death, but alas too late, who was heard oftentimes to say that now he lacked his Cromwell.* [1]

Shortly after the execution of Thomas Cromwell, three leading Protestant ministers were burned who had been sheltered by him (Barnes, Jerome and Garret – all without trial). Barnes, Coverdale's good friend and mentor, had had a chequered history since his Cambridge days as Prior of the Augustinian monks. Having escaped England after his recantation before Wolsey in 1526, and having spent long years in Germany, he was of use to Henry in his negotiations with the House of Cleves. On returning he was soon trapped by Gardiner. What particularly inflamed Gardiner was that after he had preached at Paul's Cross in February 1540, two weeks later Barnes took the same text, demonstrating the errors in Gardiner's sermon. This was intolerable and Gardiner complained to the king. On the removal and execution of Cromwell, Barnes lost his shield and was soon arrested and burned at the stake.

Burning of Robert Barnes with Garret and Jerome in 1540

At his death, Barnes gave great commendations to the king's Majesty, that he should fear God, and maintain religion, and keep marriage undefiled most honourably; and then declared his faith and his articles. Then they prayed together, and Barnes said to Master Priest, being sheriff, 'Know ye wherefore I die, seeing I was never examined nor called to any judgment?' He answered, He knew nothing, but thus we are commanded. Then he took Master Sheriff by the hand and said, 'Bear me witness, and my brother, that we die Christianly and charitably; and I pray you and all the people to pray for us: and if the dead may pray for the quick, we will pray for you.' And so he, and the rest, forgave their enemies, and kissed one another, and stood hand in hand at the stake, praying continually until the fire came: and so rested in Christ Jesus. [2]

Retreat from Bible distribution during the remainder of Henry's reign

The hostile climate for the Reformation continued with few glimpses of light through the remainder of Henry's reign. In London, in particular, Bishop Bonner was safely enthroned as Bishop of London and in 1539 had paid for six Great Bibles to be available in Paul's Cathedral for public reading. However, after the fall of Thomas Cromwell, Bonner began to change his coat with the change of weather. He now began to show a different appearance as he moved closer to Gardiner. The King was clearly moving back towards Catholicism without the Pope, and Bonner became a vocal supporter. One of his first acts, after this change of direction, was to deal with John Porter. He was a tailor who, with a strong voice, attracted a crowd to hear him read the Great Bible in St Paul's Cathedral. He was thrown into prison by Bonner where he starved to death.

The bishops and supporting noblemen were by 1542 making great complaints to the king about the English Bible. In June 1542 they had a considerable success when the sale of the Bible was stopped and referred to the bishops for amendment. Nothing materialised, but worse was to follow. In April 1543, the Act for the Advancement of True Religion forbade the reading of the Bible in public by any unlicensed person, and in private by anyone of the rank of yeoman or under, and any woman below the rank of a noblewoman. [2a]

To cap all, the Bible printers Grafton and Whitchurch were sent to prison.

Finally, six months before the death of the king, as it were to turn back the Reformation completely, a Royal Proclamation was issued to: *Avoid and abolish such English books as contain pernicious and detestable errors and heresies. As divers evil disposed persons have disseminated by books printed in English sundry pernicious errors and heresies both against the laws of the realm and repugnant to the true sense of God's word, the King ordains that no one after 31 Aug. next receive or keep the text of the New Testament of Tyndale's or Coverdale's translation, nor any English books of Frith, Tyndale, Wickliffe, Bale, Barnes, Coverdale ... Penalty for concealing such books, fine and imprisonment at the King's pleasure. No English books touching religion to be imported from abroad without special licence. (State Papers 1546)* Of the 88 books listed, twelve were from Coverdale's pen, including his 1535 Bible [3] (see Appendix 3). The Great Bible was not on the list, but no doubt some over-zealous clergymen burnt this edition too. Bishop Bonner made a huge bonfire at Paul's Cross on 26th September 1546.

Coverdale goes to Strasburg

So matters were turned back again. Priests were required to divorce their wives; some came to trial, abjured and carried faggots at Paul's Cross, while some twenty or more Reformed ministers went beyond the sea into exile again. Several considerations probably moved Coverdale to leave England in 1540. One reason would be that he had no official position in the church. Thirteen years later he was in the same position; flee or suffer. In 1553, he was one of the leading Reformed bishops and clearly believed he must stand his ground and go to his death (see Appendix 4). But in 1540, he had no official standing. He was, however, well known. He complained shortly after leaving England of his enemies continuing: *To slander me (yea, even to the King's Majesty), as though I were a perverter of the common order,*

91

or took on me to change the laws. [3a] Secondly, he must have feared compromise. Cranmer stayed at his post doing good as he was able, but there were to be many compromises ahead. Coverdale would similarly have to compromise his beliefs or share the same end as Barnes, Anne Askew and several others in the last years of Henry's reign. Finally, there was the matter of his care over his wife. The idea of having to divorce her under the Act of Six Articles would have been a strong motive to leave the country. Coverdale chose to go, though to a life of poverty and want. His knowledge of German was already very good – he had spent seven years in Germany and the Low Countries during his first exile. He left for Strasburg in 1540. It would be a further eight long years before he returned, after the death of the king. No doubt his language during those years would have been in a measure as expressed in Psalm 137 from his Ghostly Psalms and Spiritual Songs:

1 At the rivers of Babylon, there sat we down right heavily
Even when we thought upon Sion, we wept together sorrowfully
for we were in such heaviness, yea we forgat all our merriness
and left off all our sport and play. On the willow trees that were thereby
we hanged up our harps truly, And mourned sore both night and day.
2. They that took us so cruelly and led us bound into prison
required of us some melody, with words full of derision.
When we had hanged our harps away this cruel folk to us could say
Now let us hear some merry song Sing us a song of some sweet tone
as ye were wont to sing at Sion where ye have learned to sing so long.

Where should he go? His choice fell on Strasburg. The cloth trade with England, which was channelled through Antwerp, involved a number of German towns in the Rhine valley, notably Strasburg and Frankfurt. Martin Bucer, probably the most influential of the German reformers after

Luther, had persuaded the Strasburg Council to adopt the Reformation as early as 1525. It was a tolerant, open city which welcomed refugees from both France and England.

Martin Bucer: the Strasburg Reformer

However, the division in Europe between the German and Swiss churches, or more particularly between Luther and Zwingli, over the Lord's Supper was causing increasing heartache. Bucer, who tried to mediate between the two parties, tended more to Zwingli's views, but relegated them to a place of secondary importance, believing that the unity of Reformed Christians was more important than agreement on this issue. Zwingli disagreed, and shortly before his death in 1531 wrote to end their friendship. Meanwhile the division continued and widened. That Coverdale favoured the Swiss position on the Lord's Supper would appear from his preaching as early as 1527 at Steeple Bumstead. However, he was, so far as in him lay, a peacemaker. Sometime into his second exile we find a letter written by one close to him, expressing Coverdale's sadness at the strong language used by Luther against the Swiss reformers, and the widening of the breach which resulted.

It is quite likely that the Coverdales travelled to Strasburg in the company of Richard Hilles. Hilles, a London cloth merchant, gave large support to poor refugees such as Coverdale. He too had decided that England was unsafe and based himself during these years at Strasburg, conducting his trade from this base. Writing to Bullinger from Strasburg in August 1540, Hilles said: *When I perceived there was no place left for me in England unless I became a traitor to both God and man I forthwith left the country on the pretext of carrying on my trade in this place.... As I have not been indicted for heresy or summoned before the Courts of Law all my property yonder* (ie in England) *is tolerably safe... I intended going to Switzerland with my wife this present August (1540), chiefly for the sake of paying you a visit.* [3b]

A letter to Bullinger, written on 27th July 1542, from Coverdale, suggests he would have gone with Hilles to Zurich, had he been able to get there. *I have been prevented by my engagements and by a degree of bodily weakness (not to mention the narrowness of my circumstances), from making my journey to you... But what pain my absence from you causes me, I will not now attempt to describe, so briefly as I am obliged to write to you; for I am very anxious to enjoy your society, and to behold your church. Since, however, this is not permitted to me, I will patiently wait the good will of my heavenly Father* [3c] Coverdale ends the letter by commending Hilles to Bulliinger as one who was knit to him by the truth.

Instead of going to Zurich, Coverdale remained at Strasburg. From his arrival in the summer of 1540, he was active in producing and publishing several works of his own as well as turning German and Latin works of the Reformers into English.

His first achievement was make accessible to English readers Bullinger's *Old Faith*. In a letter to Bullinger shortly afterwards, Hilles says of the book: *It is much commended by those of our countrymen who favour the gospel, such as Miles Coverdale, who immediately after my arrival from England clothed it in an English dress.* [3d] In the preface Coverdale, speaking no doubt from personal experience, explained the motive which prompted him to translate this work. Speaking of England: *where there are scornful mockers, who because a man will not dance the devils dance with them, bleat out their tongues at him… There goes a fellow of the new learning, saith one, there is one of those new-fangled gospellers says another. Wherefore because the world is angry with us for our faith I have here set forth this book, partly because it showeth the antiquity of our holy Christian faith, and partly to give occasion unto all such as have received it not to shrink from any mockage or scornful derision, but to be peaceable, gentle, merciful and full of good fruits.*

Interestingly, when expelled from Geneva (1538-41) and at Bucer's invitation, John Calvin made the same choice of Strasburg in which to settle. It may well have been on his first entry to Strasburg that Coverdale became acquainted with Calvin. Just before leaving for home after this eight-year exile, Coverdale quickly rendered into German and Latin a translation of the *1548 Order of the English Communion*, sending his work to Calvin *as a token of my affection.* In the same letter, he asks Calvin to *affectionately salute your wife, who deserved so well of me and mine when we first went to Strasburg.* [4]

Calvin's talents were rapidly becoming well known through his writings by this time, although his great work in Geneva was yet to come in the twenty-four years after his return from Strasburg in 1541. In Strasburg, not only did he pastor the church of French refugees and lecture in what was soon to be called the university, but also produced an enlarged version of his Institutes of the Christian Religion.

Just as important at this stage was Calvin's first work on the Lord's Supper. Despite considerable respect for Luther, Calvin taught authoritatively that the Lord's Supper was entirely a commemorative spiritual service of remembrance. (Luther rejected the Roman Catholic doctrine of transubstantiation: *no man can at this day persuade the Papists that their mass is a great blasphemy against God, and idolatry.* [5] but believed in the *real presence*). Calvin also found fault with Luther for the sharpness used against Zwingli and the Swiss. This work of Calvin's, produced in 1540 when both he and Coverdale were in Strasburg, was soon turned into English. The Parker Society has Coverdale as the author of the English translation, and certainly it is bound with one of his other works in those copies still in existence. Coverdale would have realised the authority of this work in settling the controversy between Lutherans and Swiss, and its influence in England. Mozley suggests that the English version does not show evidence of Coverdale's style. He may be correct. However, above all, the English version reflects Calvin's plain succinct style of writing and his profound thinking.

Some modern historians, no doubt owing to a lack of enthusiasm as to the name of Calvin, have tried to distinguish between the teaching of Zwingli and Calvin on this and other matters. Their attempts lack conviction. The Swiss Reformation began to grow soon after the German one, and the division between Zwingli and Luther split the Reformation into two camps. Calvin, with the ability given him, after the death of Zwingli articulated many issues more clearly than either earlier Reformer was able to do. Among other matters, he clarified the Bible teaching on the Lord's Supper in a way satisfactory to Zwingli's successor Heinrich Bullinger who, with the other Zurich pastors, gave Calvin his support.

The split between German Lutheran churches and Swiss Reformed ones also reflected the strong insistence of Calvin that nothing should be permitted in public worship except those practices appointed in the Bible. Luther was prepared to take a more relaxed view, that anything is permitted in worship unless expressly forbidden in Scripture. A small example is that Luther's hymns became popular in public worship across Germany, but in those churches following Calvin's principles, only Psalms were permitted.

It was at this stage also that Coverdale wrote his Confutation of Sir John Standish. This man, trying to curry favour with the King, had written a scornful and derisory book against Barnes, so recently burned at the stake and whose memory was clearly sweet to Coverdale. Their association had been close from 1521 when Barnes became Prior of the Austin Friars in Cambridge and had endured through many ups and downs. Coverdale wrote scathingly of Standish: *Is it not a great worship for him to wrestle with a shadow, and to kill a dead man?* [6] Coverdale's refutation was masterly, demonstrating the emphasis the Reformers placed on the authority of Scripture. *Weakness and ignorance I can well bear, so long as it is not wilful; but the perverting or chopping up of a text of holy scripture is not to be borne unrebuked.* [7] Most important of all, Coverdale defended salvation by free grace without works and insisted that good works do not save a person before God. *But you, not regarding the order that God hath taken in the salvation of his people, turn the root of the tree upward, draw the thread through before the needle, set the cart before the horse.* [8]

It also illustrated how the reformers and the traditionalists were competing for the king's ear. Coverdale wrote: *I mourned sore within myself ... that under the king's privilege such things should be set forth, which is either against the word and truth of God or against the king's honour.* [9] This might well explain Coverdale's lament a little later in his exile when he stated that he sought *all the lawful ways that I could devise' to return to England to a greater field of usefulness, but I be hindered and kept from you by all the means that Satan and his members can imagine.* [10]

He also during his short stay in Strasburg from 1540-42, produced 'Fruitful Lessons from the Passion (Death), Burial, Resurrection and Ascension gathered out of the Four Evangelists'. The general idea was based on a work of Zwingli, but expanded and applied by Coverdale. It gave a short Bible reading, address and prayer for each day from Easter for forty days to the Lord's ascension to heaven.

At this point in time, Strasburg did not have a university, and we gather that Coverdale had a doctorate conferred on him from the University of Tubingen some fifty miles away. The university was the chief glory of the little town, and Melancthon had been one of its most distinguished teachers in past days. In 1564, Coverdale received his doctorate of Sacred Theology at Cambridge University by incorporation from Tubingen. As he went to Strasburg in 1540, and almost certainly in Denmark in 1542-3, the likely date for him to have his D.D. conferred was 1541. [11] Certainly by 1543 he was being referred to as Dr Coverdale.

This suggestion gains ground when one considers that only one work came from Coverdale's prolific pen in 1541, when in December of that year, he published a further work by Bullinger on a subject close to his heart: *The Christian state of Matrimony.* The difficulties under which the exiles lived and worked is demonstrated by this book which the printer sent out under the name of a popular English author of that time, Thomas Becon, to give it a greater sale. However, Becon himself set the record straight in 1564: *Forasmuch as a certain book treating of matrimony... was translated into our speech by the godly and gracious man Miles Coverdale, born to set forth the true Christian doctrine both by tongue and pen, it was for the more ready sale set forth in my name by the hungry printer.* [12]   No suggestion here that Coverdale was to gain any revenue from the sale of his books! Rather, the refugees were quite defenceless and open to exploitation in their exile. Two more translations from German followed from Coverdale's pen in early 1542 relating to the gathering storm of persecution, which was to break over the Lutheran churches after Luther's death.

Visit to Denmark 1542-3

From the clues available to us, we can deduce that Coverdale and his wife then went north to Denmark on a lengthy visit to her relatives. The evidence from which the dates can be identified are:

- John Foxe tells us that King Christian III of Denmark had knowledge of Coverdale when he was there in Denmark in Henry VIII's time. This limits the visit to Coverdale's second exile, as the King did not take his throne in Denmark until the last few months of the first exile.
- His brother-in-law, John Macalpine, was in 1542 appointed Professor of Divinity at Copenhagen University and chaplain to King Christian. It is reasonable to think that the visit, and the introduction to the King, was at Macalpine's initiative.
- Coverdale, after his arrival in Strasburg, was busy translating and writing. However, there is a twelve month gap from July 1542, when he neither wrote any surviving letters from Strasburg, nor produced any books.
- From September 1543 for five years, he was immersed in the busy life of a pastor and head teacher in a small town in central Germany.

- The product of his visit to Denmark was the book *The Order that the Church in Denmark doth Use*. In the preface, he tells us he had been present *long and many a day at the execution, practice and experience thereof,* suggesting a fairly lengthy visit.
- This book is on the list of those banned and burnt in 1546 in London, so must have been fairly well known in England before that date.

Copenhagen University is one of the oldest in Europe. The importance of the city was its position at the entrance of the Baltic Sea. Today the Sound is crossed by a bridge/tunnel.

There is little doubt that Coverdale wrote this work to encourage further reform in the Church of England, by recounting his experiences in Denmark, and to demonstrate how much closer they were to what he considered to be Scriptural practice. Hugh Latimer, in a sermon before King Edward VI in 1550, when he was encouraging the King and Council to further the reforms in England, made very favourable reference to this work. [13]

Pastor and teacher in Bergzabern

However, a new opportunity was now to open for Coverdale to support himself and his family, which took him back to Strasburg in 1543, probably leaving his wife with her sister in Denmark while he went to investigate. His home for the next five years was to be the small town of Bergzabern, some thirty miles north of Strasburg, as headmaster of the town school and preacher in its church. Bergzabern had an elderly minister in poor health named Nicolaus Thomae who also had charge of the town school. In May 1543, he appealed to Conrad Hubert, one of the pastors of Strasburg and a native of Bergzabern, to find him an assistant. *Who will find me, in my ill-health, a colleague, pious, learned and experienced in the things of God?* Hubert recommended Coverdale, which led to his return from Denmark, first alone and then returning with his wife once the matter was settled, beginning his labours in September 1543. Some twenty letters have been preserved from Coverdale to Hubert, detailing his life over the five years, where he served first as assistant, then after Thomae's death in 1545, as his replacement in the position of minister as well as headteacher at Bergzabern.

This small town, in the Duchy of Zweibrucken, was ruled over by seventeen-year-old Count Wolfgang, a decided Lutheran prince, who had recently come into his inheritance. His epitaph in the castle church of Meisenheim states that *he ruled his lands for 26 years confessing and defending pure gospel doctrine in perilous times, set up right teaching in his churches, abolishing idolatry, and founding schools.*[14]

Bergzabern in the Rhine-Pfalz region of Germany.
Courtesy of the Bergzabern Archive Tourismusverein SUV

Some of the letters from Coverdale to Hubert reflect the storm clouds gathering around the Lutherans in Germany. Charles V was increasingly intent on subduing the Lutherans and returning them to his religion. Kept from using force because of distracting wars with France and the Turks, it was not until 1546-7 after the death of Luther that he was able to defeat the Lutheran alliance. Meanwhile, although many of the princes of northern Germany had declared for Lutheranism, that was often a political declaration rather than one of faith. These concerns are reflected in some of Coverdale's letters to Hubert:

I went down into Lower Germany, for the purpose of bringing home my wife; yet at length upon my return, and having learned many things by experience, which during my former residence I had not sufficiently considered, I see, alas! that the present state of the churches in these parts is exceedingly calamitous, nay more, that it is absolutely deplorable. To such an extent do the princes appear to connive at the abuses which exist, the most dreadful factions to grow rife, and, what is more, the very pastors of the Lord's flock to revel in them. [15]

Nevertheless, like the diligent pastor that he was, Coverdale laboured on amidst much discouragement, with some helps as he records in one letter to Hubert. *The business of catechizing, which we attempted two previous weeks in church, we now, God be thanked, find succeed prosperously, and to be not without fruit. May God grant, that what we have begun to plant and water, may increase more and more to his glory.* (21st April 1544). *I do not doubt that the interests of religion here will daily prosper more and more; for having already experienced some proof of this, I write this, that you, who are so earnestly zealous for the church of God, may render thanks to Him for it, and unceasingly offer up your prayers for still greater success.* (13th August 1544)

Clearly too, he had cause to complain about the behaviour of his flock, many of whom had become Lutheran because their prince had done so. This is reflected in a further letter to Hubert. *The prefect invited me and my wife, as he often does, to supper on the 27th of last month. During suppertime, in the course of conversation about many matters, we happened to mention that of the sacred ministry .... The prefect on the following day, which was the Lord's day, in speaking to the people, and using very strong language, told them that he was not much pleased with some secret proceedings of our rabble.* (3rd October 1546) The burden of his flock and their carelessness was laid out in a further letter to Hubert. *The principal matter which I was desirous to have forwarded by your diligence with our prefect (for he was with you at that time at Strasburg) was this; namely, that in conformity with the duty of his office he should put a stop to those most frivolous public dances, and other hindrances of true piety of the same description; and that he should take care, that at least during the performance of the more solemn services of religion the people should conduct themselves with less irreverence; and during the time of the sermon, the prayers, and the singing, they should not collect themselves together in so many corners in every direction of the market and the burial-ground.* (6th February 1545)

Visits from Bucer and Hubert were received with great pleasure in this country district, when they were able to go. *Peace and joy in the Holy Ghost! How kind the Lord hath been to us in sending to us our dearly-beloved preceptor in Christ, Bucer, I can scarcely either declare or write, from the lively emotions of my heart. For the space of three days he displayed towards us, not without the greatest exertions, many offices both of charity and piety; by which I am assured that our churches will be not a little established in the Lord.* (22nd May 1544)

At the same time, as a good pastor Coverdale used the calamities of life, both natural and man-made, to encourage a greater trust in God. *But our little town has, alas! received very great damage from the late hail-storm, which took place eight days ago. But if we would seek for the true reason of this scourge, we must attribute it to the goodness of God, who is accustomed to chasten his adopted child, and thus invites us to repentance.* (22nd May 1544)

The darkening clouds of civil war were gathering in Germany too, as the Emperor's determination to subdue and eradicate Lutheranism from Germany began to gather pace. *For as they say the emperor is willing to admit of no peace, not even on the earnest exhortation of the princes; so it is reported, that he has just made a fresh invasion into the part of Brabant belonging to the duchy of Cleves, and the Dutch territories, with great violence. A dreadful beginning in truth! May God grant that, roused by such great evils, and truly acknowledging our great ingratitude, we may sincerely repent!* (13th August 1544) Coverdale was clear sighted

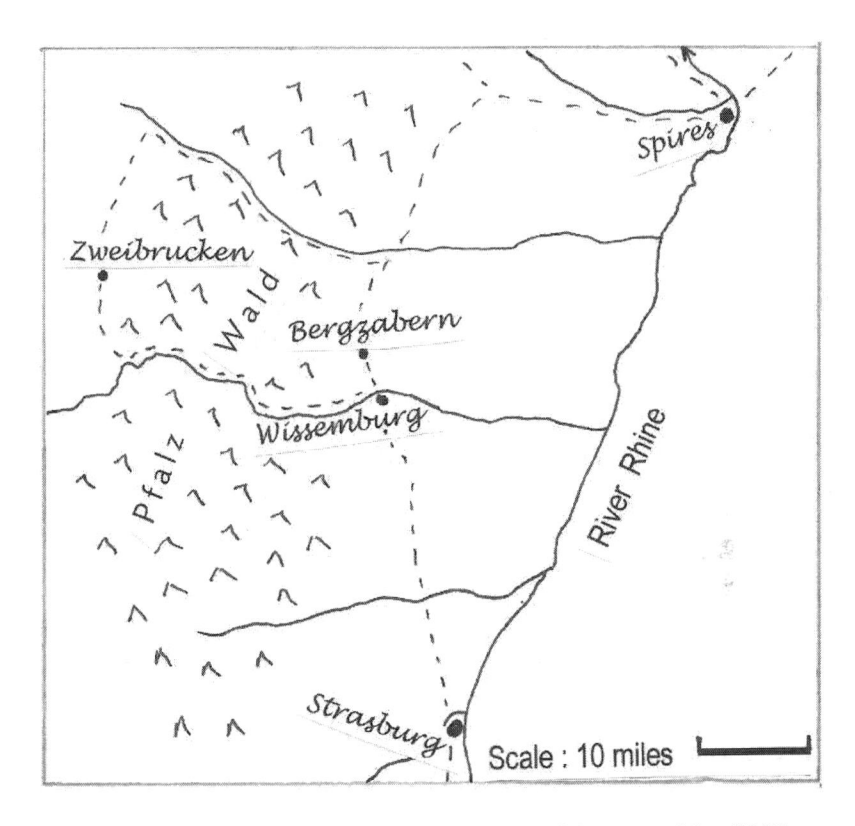

Map of Rhine Pfalz area. Today, as a result of the wars of the C20th, Bergzabern and Zweibrucken are in Germany and Strasburg and Weissemburg in France. In Coverdale's time all were German.

enough to see the way the tide was running: *I understood that Bucer, contrary indeed to the opinion of us all, had not yet returned* (the Emperor had detained Bucer in prison at Spires for a time) *at which circumstance you need not doubt that we are much grieved. But I know that the church is pleading continually with many prayers; and there is no reason for our despairing, that God, in his accustomed mercy, will set him at liberty.* (13th Sept 1544)

Coverdale also clearly struggled with poverty. No doubt he had subsisted on very little during his first three years of exile, incurring debts to those merchants such as Richard Hilles who helped to support the refugees.   In one letter, he tells Hubert: *I have also given him (the messenger who took this letter) seven florins and twelve batzen for this purpose, that, in your accustomed kindness to me, you may take care that that money be paid to my creditors; by doing which you will greatly oblige me.* (31st March 1544). That his struggles to make ends meet continued, is suggested by a further letter sent to Hubert. *That happy and illustrious youth has shewn towards me the greatest friendship, inasmuch as he not only brought the letter from you to me hither, namely, to Bergzabern, but also took upon himself the charge of conveying this money to you by a faithful messenger. It is almost impossible for me to describe in few words, how unwillingly I have detained it.* 13th April 1544 [16]

Clearly he had some influence with the Count, on whose patronage and good government he and others relied for their safety. One example is that in 1546, he was summoned to Zweibrucken, capital of the Duchy (see map), to advise on the whether an aged widowed Lutheran minister named Hilspachius should be permitted to marry a young woman of a good family. Finding it to be the evident and willing choice of both parties, Coverdale gave his approval.

In addition to his ministry, pastoral work, and his wider care for the churches in Germany, Coverdale had to run the town school. The needs here are reflected in some of his letters to Hubert. *You cannot believe, how greatly we are distressed from the want of books and the scarcity of paper.* (21st April 1544). *I intended to have inquired, and so to have ascertained from you, when I was with you at Strasburg, how and of what materials you make your ink; but owing to a press of business I omitted it. Wherefore I beg that you will either tell my wife, who is now with you, what materials I ought to procure for this purpose, or send me a list of them.* (9th Dec 1544)

In addition, Coverdale, as time permitted, continued to turn German works of divinity into English. From this reference it is also clear that Coverdale was in touch with friends in England: *And if you can by any means procure even one copy of Bucer's answer to the bishop of Winchester before the fair, I will take care that the Latin original shall be translated into English as soon as possible; which you need not doubt will be most acceptable to our brethren in the Lord throughout England. I wish, however, that it should be managed as secretly as possible, until it shall make its appearance both in Latin and English.* (February 16, 1545).

Added to other burdens was pastoral care over his flock and the citizens of the little town which also occupied Coverdale's time and energies. He writes to Hubert, whose parents and brothers still lived in Bergzabern: *But the Lord, who is always righteous in all his works, in his good pleasure deprived your brother John eight days since of that sweet child, which his wife had brought forth to him about Christmas.* (21st April 1544). When the minister of the neighbouring town of Weissemberg died, this clearly added to the work-load, some of the letters written to Hubert being written from that place.

So between the normal work of a pastor, wider troubles in Germany as they affected the Lutheran church, advising the Count, who clearly reposed increasing confidence in the counsel and advice of Coverdale, and running the school, Coverdale had little spare time during these years. *I am so overwhelmed at this time with my own affairs, that I do not write more at the present, hoping in the meantime that you will give me credit for my good intentions.* (27th December 1545) That he did not spare himself is evident from a letter from Nicolaus Thomae to Hubert on 27th April 1545, in which he writes: *I can never sufficiently thank the good and great God that by the command of our Prince, our magistrates have given me Dr Miles Coverdale as a colleague. He is a man of singular piety and incomparable diligence, a watchful and scrupulous performer of every duty of religion.* The burdens carried by Coverdale would have increased when Thomae died in the summer of 1546.

One matter which perturbed Coverdale greatly was the Lutheran view on the Lord's Supper. A letter has survived from Thomae to Hubert, written on 16th Jan 1545, which gives us some light on Coverdale's thoughts: *Coverdale and I read with astonishment that such distinguished men as Zwingli (now dead), pillars of the oppressed church should be so miserably condemned. We consider it would have been better for him* (Luther) *to have kept away from the press.... Harsh and bitter writings of this kind deter many by an insuperable obstacle. Why did we boast everywhere of agreement up to now when it seems that scholars were never more divided for a thousand years.* [17]

His time in this small corner of Germany might seem an obscure and useless five-year interval in a busy, useful life. However, this was not the view of those who knew him, as evidenced in a letter written in 1545 by Richard Hilles to Bullinger: *Myles Coverdale is truly one who is very dear to, and honourably esteemed by all the ministers of the word, and other learned men in these parts... He is the master of a grammar school in Bergzabern, where, by translating in his leisure hours, for the sake of the more extensive advancement of the kingdom of Christ various religious works into our language ... he is of very great service in promoting the scriptural benefit of those persons in the lower rank of life, who are anxious for the truth.... He is one of those who, after the example of Moses, rather choose to be banished and suffer affliction with the people of God, than with a wounded conscience to enjoy the pleasure of sin in their native Egypt.* [18]

These activities were now overtaken by two notable events that sent Coverdale back to England. The first was the death of Henry VIII at the end of January 1547, to be succeeded by nine year-old Edward VI, already showing sincere Reformed convictions. England was now safe for those exiles who had spent the years overseas since fleeing in 1540 at the enforcement of the Act of Six Articles.

The second was the victory of Charles V over the Lutherans in Germany at the battle of Muhlberg, at which the two leading Lutheran princes, the Elector of Saxony and the Landgrave of Hesse, were both captured and imprisoned. This was followed by the Augsburg Interim, an imperial decree of 15th May 1548, ordering the Lutherans to readopt traditional Roman Catholic beliefs, including the seven sacraments. It was a time of repression and discouragement for the Lutheran churches. In Strasburg, as with most other free cities now under the control of the Imperial troops, the Reformed ministers were discouraged from preaching and soon Martin Bucer and Peter Martyr, the most eminent of them, were invited to England. Germany was busy expelling friends of the Reformation; England was now welcoming them with open arms. Coverdale was back in England by the summer of 1548. A letter between two Calais merchants, now stored at Lambeth Palace Library, mentions Coverdale was to preach in that town on 14th March, suggesting that he was at that point in transit for England.

Chapter 7

The Reformation gathers pace in the days of Edward VI

Woe be unto thee (O thou realm and land) whose king is but a child, and whose princes are early at their banquets. But well is thee (O thou realm and land) whose king is come of nobles, and whose princes eat in due season, for strength and not for lust. (Ecclesiastes chapter 10 block B)

Strengthening the Reformation

The England to which Coverdale returned back in 1548, was being steered in a decidedly Reformed direction. There were various reasons for this. First, while Henry VIII had kept a careful balance in his Council, two of the most powerful men on the Roman Catholic side had crossed the old King at their peril during the last year of his life, thus tilting the Council in favour of the Reformers. The Duke of Norfolk was in the Tower as a prisoner, saved from execution only by the death of the king. Stephen Gardiner, Bishop of Winchester, had been removed from the Council after an argument over land belonging to the bishopric which the king wanted him to release. This left Edward Seymour, Duke of Somerset, in the driving seat. He became Lord Protector, and effectively ruler of the kingdom of his nine-year-old nephew Edward VI.

A second influence was the young King himself. A most remarkable letter is preserved from the King to his stepmother, Queen Katherine Parr. *Pardon my rude style in writing to you most illustrious queen and beloved mother, and receive my hearty thanks for your loving kindness to me and my sister. Yet dearest mother, the only true consolation is from heaven and the only real love is the love of God. Preserve I pray you, my dear sister Mary from all the wiles and enchantments of the evil one and beseech her to attend no longer to foreign dances and merriment which do not become a most Christian princess. And so, putting my trust in God for you to take this exhortation in good part, I commend you to His gracious keeping.* [1] The letter is dated 12 May 1546 - six months before he came to the throne! At his coronation, *when three swords were brought to be carried in the procession as emblematic of his three kingdoms, the king said 'there is one yet wanting. The Bible. That book is the sword of the spirit and to be preferred before these swords.* [2] Following this king's example to the present day, the Bible has played a significant role in the coronation service. When Queen Elizabeth II was crowned she was presented with a Bible during the service with the words *Here is Wisdom; This is the royal Law; These are the lively Oracles of God.*

Thirdly, the Church of England was now in the hands of Archbishop Cranmer who, while he had to compromise during the life of the old king, had clung on, using his influence where he could. Now, with the support of the King, the Lord Protector and a good number on the Council, he was able to move the Church of England in the direction he wanted it to go.

A useful summary of the way religious change was now to move forward is that given by MacCulloch. *This evangelical grouping knew from the start of 1547 exactly what Reformation it wanted: whatever hesitations occurred were primarily attributable to the need to disarm conservative opinion… there was an essential continuity of purpose in a graduated series of religious changes over seven years.* [3]

Portrait of Lord Protector Somerset by Holbein

The quotation captures the problem. Here was a small group of clergy and noblemen in high places, trying to move forward a nation still gripped by tradition, alongside a body of clergy mostly hostile and nobles greedily swallowing the proceeds from the closure of the monasteries. How different from the situation in Scotland thirteen years later, after John Knox returned from exile, where the most part of the Reformation in church order and government was achieved at one stroke as a result of his uncompromising boldness.

Cranmer moved forward as he felt able. In 1547, conscious of the state of the clergy, many halting between two opinions, all preaching licences were suspended. As Cranmer knew full well, there were but few ministers, especially outside of London, who gave heartfelt support to the teaching of the Reformation. Hence the suspension of preaching licences and the issue of his First Book of Homilies, twelve sermons which those priests who did not get their licences back were expected to read from the pulpit.

These homilies taught justification by faith only, and required priests to read the Bible passages appointed for each day in English. But it also allowed the priests who were the chief fomenters of opposition to the Reformation, to continue in their livings. It prescribed a form of worship sufficiently ambiguous to keep them pacified.

A Parliament was called in November 1547 which soon repealed the Act of Six Articles of Henry VIII and the severe Acts against heresies. In a further marked break with the practices of the previous reign and the next, only two were sentenced to the fire among those who opposed the religious policies of the King and Somerset. They were burned despite the vigorous protests of the boy king to Cranmer. Bishops Gardiner, Bonner and Tunstall spent the last part of the reign in prison for opposing the king's religious policies, but apart from the two burnings, that was as severe as the regime became in matters of conscience.

Injunctions were issued requiring the clergy to preach four times each year against pilgrimages and praying to images. Paintings, shrines and monuments to feigned miracles were to be taken down and every church provided with a Bible. Reformed preachers were released from prison or, as was the case with Coverdale, invited to return from exile. Permission to the clergy to marry was given and it was enacted that the Lord's Supper and other services should be administered in English.

This was the scene to which Coverdale returned with his wife in 1548 – a changed and more encouraging place of labour for those Reformed Christian ministers who had been in exile in the last years of Henry VIII. Coverdale was soon at work. The first record of his activity back in England was 24th June in London, preaching a sermon for the Merchant Taylors' Company, for which he was paid a fee of six shillings and eight pence as recorded in the company books.

Cranmer had published his Injunctions on 21st July 1547, which required not only a copy of the Bible to be placed in each parish church but also, within twelve months, a copy of the Paraphrase of Erasmus. Coverdale was mostly responsible for the English translation of the second volume of the Paraphrase, the first having been completed before his return. For the second volume, he wrote the dedication to the King and translated the epistles to Romans, Corinthians and Galatians. As this volume was published early in 1549, he must have completed the task within six months of his arrival home.

He also found time to republish Wycliffe's Wicket, against the Roman Catholic doctrine of transubstantiation. In the introduction he speaks wryly of *how many thousands of books of godly-minded men's writings have been burned in this realm since this little book was first written.* The hope he himself felt for a better future comes through. *And yet how wonderfully hath the Lord stirred up his people, even beyond all hope, unto this wonderful increase in Christian congregations.* Then he comes to the point as to why he had reissued this little work. *No one man hath more briefly and plainly declared the true understanding of the words of the Lord's Supper than did this author* (ie Wycliffe) *in this treatise following.* Many references are found in Foxe's Book of Martyrs to the usefulness of this work to those who stood their ground in the next reign when faced with certain death by burning. This one point of their faith more than any other attracted the wrath of the Marian authorities.

There was a big rise in Reformed and Lutheran printing activity at this time, including English translations of the works of Calvin and Luther. The number of books printed rose to 267 in 1548, the highest total for some years (15% being by those two authors). The government did not authorise this, but did encourage it. Coverdale was at the forefront of such work.

Chaplain to Queen Katherine Parr and to the King

By the summer of 1548, Coverdale was also almoner to Dowager (widowed) Queen Katherine Parr. This office made him responsible for her charitable giving to the poor. Evidence suggests he also acted as a chaplain to her household. She, being the sixth wife of Henry VIII, had become a decided Reformer.

The Dowager Queen had married Admiral Thomas Seymour, an uncle to Edward VI and brother to Lord Protector Somerset, after the death of Henry VIII, and was now with child. She spent the summer at Sudeley Castle in Gloucestershire, with a retinue of over one hundred gentlemen and yeomen of the guard, and with Lady Jane Grey who lived under her guardianship at this time. Coverdale, no doubt with the other ministers in her service, took the twice daily service in the castle chapel. This soon came to an end with the death of Katherine Parr on 5th September 1548, having given birth to a living daughter.

Sudeley Castle, Gloucestershire. The church containing the tomb of Queen Katherine Parr is in the foreground. Photograph courtesy of the Family.

A record of the funeral is preserved among the manuscripts of the College of Heralds: *First came Somerset herald, then the corpse borne by six gentlemen in black gowns... followed by the Lady Jane Grey as chief mourner.... Dr Coverdale, the Queen's almoner began his sermon, which was very good and godly, and in one place he took occasion to declare how no one there should think, say, or spread it abroad that the offering was done to benefit the dead, but only for the poor, and that the lights which stood about the corpse were for no other intent or purpose than the honour of the person'.* A recent injunction had required ministers to explain to their hearers that *whereas they had been diligent to bestow much substance upon pardons, trentals, candles and other blind devotions, they were now to give alms for the relief of the poor.*

The Book of Common Prayer

We next find Coverdale at Windsor Castle during the Autumn of 1548. He was appointed chaplain to the King [5] and was one of the group of divines at work there framing the Prayer Book. The number of Reformed bishops and preachers was still very small compared with the number of bishops and preachers who favoured the old religion, so no doubt Cranmer wanted all the help he could get. This was the first real attempt to change the services in the Church of England, beyond the hesitant and halting efforts of Cranmer during the late king's reign. By the First Act of Uniformity, which passed both houses of Parliament in January 1549, the Book of Common Prayer was declared to be the only legal service book in England and Wales. A measure of Cranmer's difficulties was the opposition of many of the bishops. When the Bill to replace the old missals with the Prayer Book came before Parliament, only six bishops voted for it, five against, sixteen absent – mostly hostile, but not willing to be seen to be opposing the King, Protector and Archbishop.

The Prayer Book was a step forward in the Reformation. The language in the Prayer Book changed from Latin to English, so that *the people might understand and have profit from hearing,* and the emphasis was on active participation by members of the congregation, to endorse the Reformed doctrine of the priesthood of all believers. *It included much that was familiar, and left a good deal that was optional, such as kneeling, crossing, holding up of hands, knocking on the breast and other gestures.* [6] Cranmer moved as far as he dared, conscious of the lack of acceptance of the new order both among the clergy and the common people. Gone was the Latin service, the Mass and the use of penance. In their place came an emphasis on regular reading of the Scriptures in English from Coverdale's Great Bible, a Communion Service once per week to encourage all to come to church (with the laity taking bread and wine), and a reduction in the number of Saints' days from approximately 180 down to 25.

However, the Book of Common Prayer came short of the expectations of the Reformers. Martin Bucer, in his book 'Censura', found 60 flaws. Most seriously, the 'Order of Communion' could be used in a similar way to the old Mass and often was, by those clergy resistant to change – by elevating the bread while the people knelt, and chanting in the same manner as before. Cranmer, whose project it was, was fearful of moving too far too fast. Bucer, having met Cranmer, reported back to his friends in Strasburg: *Some concessions have been made both to a respect for antiquity, and to the infirmity of the present age; such as for instance, the vestments commonly used in the sacrament of the eucharist, and the use of candles, so also in regard to the commemoration of the dead ... They are only to be retained for a time, lest the people, not yet thoroughly instructed in Christ, should by too extensive innovations be frightened away from Christ's religion.* [7]

Even at the start these cautious steps caused strife on both sides and were to do so throughout the next 140 years, as the Reformation movement in England grew and spread. While on the one side the vast majority of the priests came on board reluctantly, on the other hand, the likes of Hooper, Rogers and Coverdale had been to Switzerland and Germany where the Reformation had travelled much further than Cranmer and Ridley were willing to go. One hundred years later John Owen, in defending the nonconformist refusal to take part in the worship of the Church of England, looking back had this to say: *God having been pleased to send the saving light of the gospel into the minds and hearts of them in chief rule – that is King Edward and some of his councillors – they found no small difficulties to wrestle with in dealing with the inveterate prejudices of the generality of men were possessed against the work they intended. The greater part of the clergy with all their might and cunning opposed their endeavours. The greatest part of the nobility averse to their proceedings; the body of the people blinded with superstition and profaneness and foreign nations round about fomenting to the utmost all home-bred discontents.' So it was hard work for the king and his councillors to facilitate the work of Reformation, especially as the ordinary people were ignorant of the Scriptures. So inflamed were the generality of the people, with the priests ready to blow on the coals, that the Reformers who had the chief responsibility decided to temporise. The Book of Common Prayer became from its very cradle and infancy a bone of contention to the church of God in this nation.* [8]

While at Windsor, Coverdale wrote, on 21st October, to his friend Paul Fagius who was struggling on at Strasburg under the heel of Emperor Charles, *with exceeding great compassion for those whom this dreadful tyranny so greatly distresses.* Coverdale gave him a warm invitation on behalf of Cranmer to come over to England to help the work of Reformation, if he felt his usefulness had come to an end in Strasburg. As Coverdale had anticipated, the Strasburg Council were forced to dismiss Fagius and Bucer in March 1549, upon which both men came to England to help forward the Reformation, Fagius going to join Peter Martyr in teaching at Oxford University, where he soon died.

When Martin Bucer arrived in England Cranmer took him to meet Edward VI. Bucer certainly had a high opinion of him and wrote to his friends of his impressions: *The king is godly and learned to a miracle; he is well acquainted with Latin and has a fair knowledge of Greek… but no study delights him more than that of Holy Scripture, of which he daily reads about ten chapters with the greatest attention.* [9]

Statue at Windsor Castle of Edward VI reading his Bible.

Bucer was a shrewd observer of the English scene. Having been introduced to the king by Cranmer, who knew his worth, he was appointed Professor of Divinity at Cambridge University. His teaching soon settled the controversies concerning justification by faith only which had been raging at the university. He wrote an illuminating letter to Calvin on 25th May 1550 concerning the wrongs in the English church: *The clergy uneducated, pluralities, many congregations had had no sermons for years, university professors either Episcopalian or Roman Catholic, noblemen enriching themselves, and bishops claiming they could do nothing without the support of the government.'* His conclusion: *it is greatly to be feared that the dreadful wrath of God will shortly blaze forth against this kingdom also.* [10] Bucer only lived two years after his arrival in England dying on 28th February 1551. Edward VI in his Chronicle records that at his funeral 3000 people, almost the whole of Cambridge, town and gown, followed him to the grave.

During the first part of 1549 Coverdale was in London about his usual work of preaching and writing, as we find him three times preaching at Paul's Cross. The first occasion was when the Mass was abolished at St Paul's Cathedral on 17th March, Coverdale was invited to preach in the presence of a large number of clergy, dignitaries and a very large congregation of Londoners (the congregation at Paul's Cross outside the cathedral was sometimes estimated at 6,000). Again on 27th April, he was requested to preach. On this occasion, two men had been required to abjure and 'carry the faggot' – some things had not yet been reformed! No doubt Coverdale, to the best of his ability, gave an explanation of the truths as taught in Scripture. The third occasion was on 10th June, the day after the issue of the new Prayer Book for use throughout the kingdom.

The Prayer Book Rebellion in Devon and Cornwall

In Devon and Cornwall in 1549 came the most serious outbreak of armed opposition to the government of Edward VI, the Prayer Book rebellion. This had deeper roots than the Prayer Book. By 1549 the government of England was in deep trouble. While the country was Protestant at the top, and none more so than the boy king and his fervent preachers, it was being misruled. The Duke of Somerset had the government in his hand. To support the English interest in Scotland, and the Protestant party there, the Protector decided to invade Scotland to try to oust the French party there. But as soon as the English army set foot in Scotland, all parties united against the invader! Things soon got worse. Advancing close to Edinburgh, the English army gave battle to the countrymen who had flocked to the Scottish banner. The result was an overwhelming victory for the English at Pinkie Cleugh. Some 14,000 Scots were slain on the field and in the pursuit. This was hardly the way to encourage Scotland to a favourable view of the English.

The war with Scotland proved ruinously expensive and the English army soon withdrew. In three years the government spent £1.5m, much of it on war in Scotland and France. The revenue of the state in that time was £0.3m. Furthermore, an offended Scottish nobility sent Mary, the Scottish child Queen, to France for her training, which was to bind them more closely to French interests. The French also won back Boulogne thus reducing the English to a small toehold around Calais, and sent an army into Scotland. To make matters worse, Somerset continued the practice of the last four years of the previous reign, by debasing the currency to help pay the government's expenses. When this proved insufficient, in desperation loans were raised from the Antwerp bankers and moneylenders at 13-14% interest.

The church lands could have helped to pay the debts. During the last four years of Henry VIII, the remaining ecclesiastical property was being transferred to the state and this process was work in progress when Henry VIII died. The Protector was authorized by Parliament to complete the sales to provide schools, hospitals and provision for the clergy. Many of the nobles, with the Lord Protector at the head, began to enrich themselves at bargain prices. *The carcass was cast out into the field, and the vultures of all breeds and orders flocked to the banquet.* [11] When the time of reckoning came to Protector Somerset it was estimated that church lands had been sold for £350,000; those given away were worth £730,000; and those stolen by ministers of the Crown and their friends £500,000. [11]

A further calamity was enclosure. The high price obtained for sheep tempted greedy landowners to dispossess the labourers and enclose the common land, reducing many of the poorest to beggary and distress. As inflation took hold and as less corn was being grown, the price of corn and bread shot up. The condition of many country districts was becoming critical. Only a spark was needed to set large areas on fire. That spark in Devon and Cornwall was the introduction of the Prayer Book in June 1549.

In 1549 there broke out peasant rebellions in various parts of the country. The Duke of Somerset, with the Scottish war unravelling, had not the resources of soldiers or money for a brutal crackdown. The complaints of peasants were of the hardship, hunger and poverty which the government was inflicting on them. However, the rebellion in Devon and Cornwall also had a religious overtone. Among the demands of the rebels were the restoration of the Act of Six Articles, the withdrawal of the Prayer Book and the restoration of the Mass. The rebellion grew in strength until some ten thousand had gathered together, imprisoning some of the gentry, and advancing through the whole of Devon and Cornwall without opposition until they reached Exeter. While they had many sympathisers within the walls, the town officials, led by the mayor, shut the gates and organised for defence. The rebels lay siege to Exeter on 2nd July.

Lord John Russell, 1st Earl of Bedford and Lord Privy Seal, was sent by the Council to deal with the Prayer Book rebellion. Preachers were to go with him to instruct the people. It would seem the only one who agreed to go was Coverdale. *Such as must be content patiently to bear those odious names of puritan or precision have yet been the men who most faithfully in their calling, have served their country both within the realm and without, in garrison and field, hazarding their bodies against harquebus and cannon. For proof hereof if you call to remembrance who hazarded his life with the Earl of Bedford when he went to subdue the Popish rebels in the West, you shall find that none of the clergy both out of pulpits and other places, would not in any such service of the Prince and country be seen, but only old father Coverdale.* [12]

Exeter City wall, much of which stands to this day, kept out the rebel army during a five week siege.

Lord Russell found himself in deep trouble by the time he reached Honiton, not having the money to pay his soldiers, who began to desert. It was at this critical point three merchants furnished Lord Russell with the money to carry on. One, John Bodley, was to become a firm friend of Coverdale. A second was Thomas Prestwood, later to be three times mayor of Exeter. Hooker tells us: *He was very zealous in religion ... and very friendly to all good preachers but especially to Mr Coverdale. He followed the Lord Russell in person and aided him with his purse.* [13] A series of battles took place over several days, at Fenny Bridges, Woodbury Windmill, Clyst St Mary and Topsham Road, as the King's army fought its way from Honiton to Exeter. After one of these battles, which took place on a Sunday, it is recorded that, *where after the victory was gotton, Miles Coverdale then a preacher and attending upon my Lord in this journey made a sermon and caused a general thanksgiving to be made unto God.* [14] Lord Russell marched into Exeter, relieving the siege of the town on 6th August 1549.

It had been a close run matter. Exeter had been the only town in Devon and Cornwall which had held out for the king. Hooker, a young man living in the town through the siege, speaks of two parties in the town *the one and greater number were of the old stamp and of the Romish religion. The other being of the lesser number were of the contrary mind and disposition for they wholly applied themselves to the reformed religion.* [15] Various attempts at treachery were discovered during the five week siege of the town, including attempts made to open the gates to the rebels, while the besiegers tried to undermine the walls by digging tunnels and cannonaded the streets from the local heights. These events, together with the shortage of food in the besieged town, made Hooker's conclusion more striking: *so in the end it came to no effect, because the Lord kept the city.* [16]

Lord Russell and his army left Exeter on 25th September, having meted out harsh punishment on many of the ringleaders of the rebellion and others. Rose-Troup reckons that with the deaths over several days in the fighting outside Exeter, and the executions, some 5,000 rebels died.

It would seem Coverdale stayed on, preaching and teaching, to try to bring the people to a better understanding of the changes made in religion. It would have been dangerous and difficult work. Some four months later, on 5th February 1550, Bishop Hooper, who came from the West country, was still unable to visit his parents: *by reason of the frequent and dangerous commotions stirred up in those parts on account of religion, and which are indeed not yet calmly and quietly settled ... the people is still wincing, by the inveiglements of the bishops, and the malice of the mass-priests.* [17]

By the Autumn, Protector Somerset had lost the support of the Council as a result of the parlous state of the country. John Dudley, Duke of Northumberland, now became Lord President of the Council. He continued state policy in a Reformed direction. He could hardly have done otherwise against the wishes of the king, Cranmer and other nobles. He made peace with Scotland and France and stabilised the currency. Just before the fall of Somerset, one of his most loyal supporters in Council, Sir Edward Paget wrote him a frank and perceptive letter: *Society in a realm doth consist and is maintained by religion and law, and these two lacking, farewell to all just society, government and justice. I fear at home is neither. The use of the old religion is forbidden and the use of the new is not yet printed in the stomachs of 11/12 parts of the realm.* [18]

On 11th October 1549 Somerset was committed prisoner to the Tower of London by order of his fellow councillors, where he remained until 6th February 1550. While there, Coverdale translated for him a German tract, *A Spiritual and most precious Pearl*, whose preamble states that *it is designed to teach all men to love and embrace the cross as a most sweet and necessary thing unto the soul, and what comfort is to be taken thereof.* The Duke of Somerset records: *In our great trouble which of late did happen unto us, as all the world doth know, when it pleased God for a time to attempt us with his scourge, and to prove if we loved him, in reading this book we found great comfort, and an inward and godly working power, much relieving the grief of our mind.* [19]   As a result, the Duke had the work published in May 1550 so others could profit as he felt to have done.

A further labour of Coverdale in 1550 was the reprinting of the 1535 Bible, this time a smaller quarto edition similar to the third edition, suitable to be carried to and from church or studied by individuals.   This was a step forward from the pulpit folio size Bibles of 1535 and the Great Bible of 1539, and demonstrates the importance given at this stage to the further step of a wider spread of Bible reading in the home. This edition was printed at Zurich, and Coverdale dedicated it to Edward VI.

Considering now most gracious prince the inestimable treasure fruit and prosperity everlasting, that God giveth with His Word, and trusting in his infinite goodness that he would bring my simple and rude labour herein to good effect, therefore was I emboldened in God sixteen years ago, not only to labour faithfully in the same, but also in most humble wise, to dedicate this my poor translation to your graces most noble father: ... most humbly beseeching the same that though this volume be small and not wholly the text appointed for the churches (ie not the Great Bible), *it may yet be exercised in all other places, so long as it is used within the company of the fear of God and due obedience unto your most excellent majesty, whom the same eternal God save and prefer evermore, Amen*

Chapter 8

Bishop of Exeter

And when the king (Josiah) heard the words of the law he rent his clothes. And the king commanded... and said: go your way, ask counsel at the Lord for me and for the remnant in Israel and for Judah, concerning these words of the book that is found. For great is the indignation of the Lord that is gone forth over us, because our fathers have not kept the word of the Lord, to do according as it is written in this book. (2 Chronicles 34 block D)

Appointed Bishop

Coverdale, seeing the great need, stayed on in Devon, preaching far and wide. It was his strong belief that instruction in the principles of the Bible would pacify and make loyal citizens in the West Country far more than would sword and fire. His labours were not unnoticed. Preaching at Court in March 1550 on the Parable of the Good Samaritan, among other remarks, Latimer referred to Coverdale's hazardous labours in Devon. Having likened the absentee bishop, John Vesey, to the Levite who passed by on the other side, refusing to see the misery before him, Latimer said *'now who was neighbour to this wounded man? He that did the office of a neighbour he was neighbour... Who is Bishop of Exeter, forsooth, Master Coverdale.* [1] Vesey was an elderly man, an absentee bishop living in Worcestershire, who had systematically impoverished the diocese. Strype tells us that the bishopric of Exeter was valued at £1565/yr in the time of Vesey, but by July 1553 only £500.[2]   Hooker records that Vesey had 32 lordships and manors left to him, but left to his successors not above three or four.[3]

Strype tells us that, though a Reformation bishop was needed in Exeter at this critical time, the Council proceeded with caution.   Vesey had been chaplain to Henry VIII, governor of Princess Mary, and had taken part in the consecration of Cranmer.   However, with some judicial pressure, he was made willing to resign through the instrumentality of Lord Russell.   The £500 needed to pay the first fruits to the Crown when Coverdale was made bishop he could not find, having returned from Germany in great poverty.   So at Cranmer's request they were not required of him, nor the arrears due from Vesey's years. Coverdale no doubt had enough of an uphill struggle on his hands without the constant worries of the debts owed by his predecessor to the Crown.

We are told *he was an excellent and able preacher of the gospel and therefore judged very fit to govern the church and to preach in the western parts much overrun with popery and ignorance, and to settle matters of religion there after a dangerous rebellion.*[3a]

A little light is shed on this uphill struggle from a survey carried out on the state of the clergy in the neighbouring diocese of Gloucester in 1551.   John Hooper, the bishop, found that out of 311 clergy, 168 were unable to repeat the Ten Commandments, 40 could not tell where in the Bible the Lord's Prayer is to be found, and of these 40, 31 did not know who was the author of the Lord's Prayer.[4]   Also we are told that, although the canons of Exeter Cathedral, no doubt dutifully, read the homilies and used the Book of Common Prayer, *their devotion to popish superstitions was in no wise abated, for on Mary's accession, they openly rejoiced.*[5]

Even in Exeter itself matters were not easy for Coverdale though there was a determined and influential party who remained loyal to Crown and the Reformation. No doubt these would have supported Coverdale through these years of labour in Devon and Cornwall. Some five years later, we find Exeter merchants, John Bodley and William Kethe in exile in Geneva together during the reign of Mary. These were strong adherents to Coverdale's Reformation principles. The party would also include many members of the guilds and some of the seafaring men. Certainly there must have been a loyal core of those favouring the Reformation. By the time of the Armada of 1588, there was a strong body of seamen from these Devon ports who served against the power of Spain in its attempts to bring England back to the old religion by invasion and force of arms.

Exeter Cathedral

We find Coverdale absent from his arduous labours in Devon on 7rd March 1551, when he preached at Westminster Abbey at the funeral of Lord Wentworth, Lord Chamberlain and thus a member of the royal household and a member of the Privy Council. While in London, Coverdale performed another and much less happy duty. This was to take part as translator and judge in the trial of George van Parris, a German member of the Strangers' Church, who was tried for heresy on 6-7th April 1551. His error was to deny the divinity of the Lord Jesus Christ. While the other judges, Cranmer and Ridley favoured burning at the stake as a punishment for such views, it is not clear whether Coverdale shared them. Given his mild disposition, it is possible that he inclined more to the principled opposition of John Foxe to such punishment. We are told he acted as translator out of the German during the trial, but there is no record of how he voted as judge. Van Parris was the second and last person to be burned for heresy during the reign of Edward VI.

From here he spent a few days with Peter Martyr at Oxford. To Martyr's great grief Martin Bucer had died a few weeks previously. Martyr poured out his grief to his Strasburg friend Conrad Hubert: *I am so broken and dismayed ... scarcely able to retain my senses by the bitterness of my grief. Oh wretched me, as long as Bucer was in England, I never felt to be in exile. But now I am alone.* Martyr was surrounded with opposition at Oxford, and Coverdale and Hooper spent a few days with him there in the Spring of 1551. *Our common friend the Bishop of Gloucester is gone down to his bishopric, actively engaged in preaching to the flock and has a numerous and attentive congregation. He was with me at Oxford for three days before Easter, together with Michael Coverdale, a most effective preacher, and one who deserves well of the gospel. Both of them preached to our people at Oxford.* Peter Martyr in another letter went further. In writing to Bullinger on 1st June, he said: *there is an excellent man, Michael Coverdale, who for some years had charge of a parish in Germany. He is actively engaged in Devonshire both in preaching and interpreting the Scripture. You are, I think, well acquainted with him. He is to be made Bishop of Exeter. Nothing can be more conducive to reformation of religion than the advancement of such men to the government of the church.* In fact it took longer to lever Vesey out of his comfortable chair than these good men expected, but on 20th June 1550 Coverdale received £40, a large sum, from the Privy Council in gratitude for his labours, and was made Coadjutor to the Bishop of Exeter. (Acts of Privy Council).

By August 1551 Vesey had been deposed and Coverdale was made Bishop of Exeter. Strype tells us that there were long delays, partly from the sweating sickness which was rather serious at this time, partly due to affairs of state, and partly because of Coverdale's enemies. So much so, that Archbishop Cranmer wrote to Secretary Cecil on 23rd August 1551: *The bearer hereof Mr Coverdale, bishop-elect of Exeter, is now through in all matters as to the consecration, save only in doing his homage and in the dispatch of the first fruits, these shall be heartily to desire that in consideration of his long attendance and the great lack the west parts have of him, you will show him your accostomable favour at this time, that by your procurement he may sooner take his oath and have your gentle assistance to the obtaining of his suit concerning the firstfruits…* Cecil acted immediately and Coverdale took the oath and paid his homage to the king on 27th August.

Coverdale's Coat of arms when Bishop of Exeter

Three days later, on 30th August, he was consecrated as Bishop of Exeter at the Archbishop's palace in Croydon, wearing surplice and cope. Losing no time, on the 11th September he was enthroned in Exeter Cathedral. He was authorised by Royal Patent, to *ordain and deprive ministers, confer benefices, appoint officials, visit the clergy, punish scandalous persons, and deal with all other parts of the episcopal function according to the word of God and in the name of the king.*

He at once carried on where he had left off his labours of the previous two years, beginning a visitation of his vast diocese; the whole of Devon and Cornwall. There is record of him at Bodmin, Padstow, Totnes and other parts of the recently rebellious region. No doubt he would have stopped and preached at the parish church of each main town to the gentry, merchants, seadogs and yeomen who gathered. However, what could one man do, when he had to supervise nearly 700 parishes? He needed the help of sound preachers. But where would he find them? His Diocesan register records that he ordained ten applicants to the ministry and instituted 47 to livings during his two years as bishop.

Hooker's description of Coverdale carries weight on account of his familiarity with the bishop, in whose household he lived for a time: *He preached continually upon every holy day ... He was a great keeper of hospitality, very sober in diet, godly in life, friendly to the godly, liberal to the poor, and courteous to all men, void of pride, full of humility, abhorring covetousness, and an enemy to all wickedness and to wicked men whose company he shunned and whom he would in no wise shroud or have in his house and company. There was no one person, being in his house, which did not from time to time give an account of his religion, and also live accordingly.* [8]

To free himself from administrative burdens so he could preach and teach, Coverdale sent to Oxford for Robert

Weston, a distinguished lawyer and loyal friend, who became his Chancellor.

And because himself was not skilful therein, neither would be hindered from his godly studies, nor encumbered with worldly matters; and yet judging it meet that the Government should be carried on with all justice and equity, he sent to Oxford for a learned man to be his Chancellor; and by the assistance of his Friends, he obtained Mr Robert Weston Doctor of the Civil Law (and afterwards Lord Chancellor in Ireland) *unto whose fidelity he committed his Consistory, and the whole charge of his Ecclesiastical jurisdiction, allowing him - not only all the Fees belonging thereto, but also lodged, and found him, his Wife, and Family, horse and man within his own House, and gave him a pension of £40 per annum besides, which was a very great matter in those days; so liberal was this good Bishop in the allowance which he made to this good Chancellor. And surely the Bishop was no more godly and careful in performing his Office of preaching, than his Chancellor was diligent, strict and just in doing of his Office without the reproach of partiality or bribery.* [9]

He was surrounded with mountains of difficulty on every side during this brief period. One perplexity was the hostility of many of the clergy and people who had been behind the Prayer Book rebellion. John Hooker tells us:

Notwithstanding this good man was a blameless bishop and lived most godly and virtuous, yet the common people, those old bottles that would receive no new wine, could not brook nor digest him for no other cause but because he was a preacher of the gospel, an enemy to papistry and a blameless man. Many devices were accounted against him for his confusion, sometimes by railings and false libels, sometimes by secret backbitings, and in the end practised his death by poisoning, both at Bodmin and Totnes by unseasonable and corrupted drinks. But by the Providence of God the snares were broken and he, simple as a dove, was delivered. [10]

Two of those clergymen who bitterly opposed Coverdale were required in 1552 to make public recantation in the cathedral. These two were John Pollard, Archdeacon of Barnstaple and Walter Hele, Vicar of Ipplepen. Hele's thirteen page confession tells us that he had openly defied and insulted the bishop when examined by order of the Privy Council.

The House of Lords

One of Coverdale's responsibilities was to sit in the House of Lords. He took his seat for the last four months of this first Edwardian Parliament, from 23rd January to 15th April 1552, and he is recorded in the House of Lords Journal as being in his seat for all except two of the 54 sessions. No doubt his first sitting would have been tinged with sadness as the day before the Duke of Somerset had been executed on Tower Hill. Somerset, a friend to the Reformers, was hurried to his death on felony charges, but many suspected it was to allow the Duke of Northumberland to consolidate his grip on power. Cranmer's attempts to save Somerset's life caused a rift with Northumberland which, over the next two years, was to grow wider.

Archbishop Cranmer was steadily pushing forward his reforms and Coverdale loyally supported him in measures which moved the Church of England away from tradition towards the Bible-based services which were a hallmark of the Reformation. His dissent, along with that of Cranmer and three other bishops, was recorded against a Bill regarding buying and selling of offices. He was also appointed to a committee to examine the Bill which became the 1552 Act for the Provision and Relief of the Poor. The most important three measures, however, were the reform of Ecclesiastical laws, revised Articles of Faith, and the 1552 Prayer Book.

The first of these measures, the reform of Ecclesiastical laws was unsuccessful, it was unfinished work at the death of the King. It involved Coverdale in a considerable outlay of time as he was appointed to the committee of bishops, one of the four committees which was to scrutinise this measure. [10a] At last Cranmer had a good number of bishops who sympathised with him. In addition, Convocation sat at the same time as Parliament and debated and accepted a further measure of Cranmer's. This was a statement of beliefs: the 42 articles of religion of the Church of England (reduced to 39 eight years later), which gained the sanction of the King in Council.

Finally, the Prayer Book was approved by Parliament and reissued in 1552 by Cranmer. The increasingly Reformed nature of the bench of bishops was demonstrated in that of twelve bishops present at the Third Reading (including Coverdale), only two (Norwich and Carlisle) voted against. It was a further significant step towards a Reformed Church, having dropped the doctrine of transubstantiation. Exorcism, prayers for the dead, auricular confession and the use of the cross in communion services were also removed and the words to be used in the distribution of bread became more Scriptural. Ridley, who had been appointed Bishop of London in 1550, was right-hand man to Cranmer in dealing with these issues.

Congregations of Dutch and German exiles as well as groups of French and Italian refugees came to England. Matters were becoming more difficult, especially in Germany with the victories of the Emperor over the Lutherans and his attempts to impose Roman Catholic teaching on them. These who came to London were permitted their own churches and form of Protestant worship. The best known, the Church of the Strangers, was formed in London with the king's permission. The congregation numbered some 5000 and called John Lasco to be their pastor in 1550. It is commonly suggested that Cranmer actively encouraged this church as a spur to the half-reformed Church of England on the one hand, but kept a firm check on it to prevent too much controversy on the other hand.

This was the first church in England actively to practise congregational singing, something Coverdale had gently encouraged, both with the issue of his 'Ghostly Psalms and Hymns' in 1535 and by describing the order of the churches in Denmark and Germany. The order of service written by John Lasco contained the following instruction: *After the Lord's Prayer is finished, by order of the minister a psalm is begun by persons specifically appointed for the purpose with a view to avoiding confusion in the singing, the whole congregation soon joining the singing with the utmost propriety and dignity.* [10b]

Coverdale was appointed by the House of Lords in 1552 to a commission of four bishops to oversee the Strangers' Church. The others were Ridley, Hooper and Thirlby (traditionalist bishop of Norwich, who reverted to Roman Catholicism in Queen Mary's reign). No doubt Coverdale's German was useful, but the issue of how fast to move forward the Church of England would no doubt have been uppermost in Cranmer's mind, with Coverdale and Hooper both keen to use the practice of the Stranger's Church to encourage further reform to the Church of England.

This Parliament had sat for nearly five years and had been convened by the Duke of Somerset at the start of the reign. The Duke of Northumberland felt Parliament had served its time, and on 15th April 1552, the king made an entry into his diary: *Parliament broke up and, because I was sick and not able to go abroad, I signed a Bill containing the names of the Acts I would pass.*

A second Parliament of the reign was called a year later. At the first sitting on 1st March 1553, the king being unwell and unable to travel the short distance to Parliament, he required Bishop Ridley to preach and Parliament to attend him. It was this sermon which moved the king to ask the bishop what he could do to further the cause of the poor. The result was the endowment of St Thomas' Hospital, Christ's Hospital School, and Bridewell prison – two of which organisations remain to this day.   This Parliament was dissolved on the last day of March 1553, having sat for only 22 days, with Coverdale again present for each sitting except one.   Little was achieved.   There was now increasing tension between the Duke of Northumberland and the Reformed party, which effectively put an end to any further progress in reform of religion.   Cranmer objected strongly to the sale of church and chantry lands for the enrichment of the nobility.   Northumberland, effectively the ruler of England, was using it as a vehicle to enlarge his power and patronage.

Thomas Cranmer: Archbishop of Canterbury 1533-53

This second short Parliament effectively ended in stalemate between the two parties.   Bradford, Lever, Ridley and John Knox all preached before the king and court during this time, and all were on record for their uncompromising reproofs to the courtiers and nobles around the king.   John Knox was in England from 1549 after his release from the slavery of the French galleys, preaching at Berwick and Newcastle and then being appointed one of six chaplains to the king. In his last sermon before the frail fifteen-year-old king he roundly reproved the covetous and time-serving princes and noblemen surrounding Edward. *What wonder that a young and innocent king be deceived by crafty covetous wicked and ungodly counsellors? I am afraid greatly that Ahithophel be counsellor, that Judas bear the purse and Shebna be scribe.* [11] Knox was summoned before the Council on 14th April. Rather than complain about the sermon, knowing the favour the king had to him, the Councillors brought against him his refusal of a bishopric, his objections to the 1552 Prayer Book and to kneeling at the sacrament. When they dismissed him, saying that *they were sorry to understand he was of a contrary mind to the common order,* Knox, unabashed, replied that *he was more sorry that the common order should be contrary to Christ's institutions'.*

In any case, all efforts of the preachers at further reform came to an abrupt end. On 6th July 1553 Edward VI died. In a letter Calvin wrote to a friend a few days later, he wrote: *that most pious king of England departed to the Lord on 6th July – and he departed very happily indeed with a holy confession. The book which I here send you was written by him and published in the month of May. You will see from it how great a treasure the Church of Christ hath lost.* [12] (The work cited is *Against the Primacy of the Pope* by Edward VI, published May 1553). At the end of Edward's life, conscious that all he had done would now be undone if his sister Mary became queen, he put in place a scheme for his cousin Lady Jane Grey, his childhood companion and lower in line to the throne, after his two sisters and Mary Queen of Scots, to succeed him. However, Henry VIII's will was quite explicit. Edward VI was to be succeeded first by Mary his older sister, and if she died without issue, by his sister Elizabeth. Edward's difficulty was that Mary was a staunch Roman Catholic. Crucially, his Council did not secure the person of Mary before proclaiming Lady Jane Grey to be queen. Mary, keeping her ear to the ground, fled to Suffolk out of reach. After nine days, the new regime collapsed, Lady Jane Grey, her husband and her father-in-law, the Duke of Northumberland were sent to the Tower and Mary rode into London in triumph.

Cranmer immediately settled all his debts, paid off his servants and ordered his affairs. It is said by Foxe that he

Tudor Family Tree
(The five Tudor monarchs reigned for 118 years)

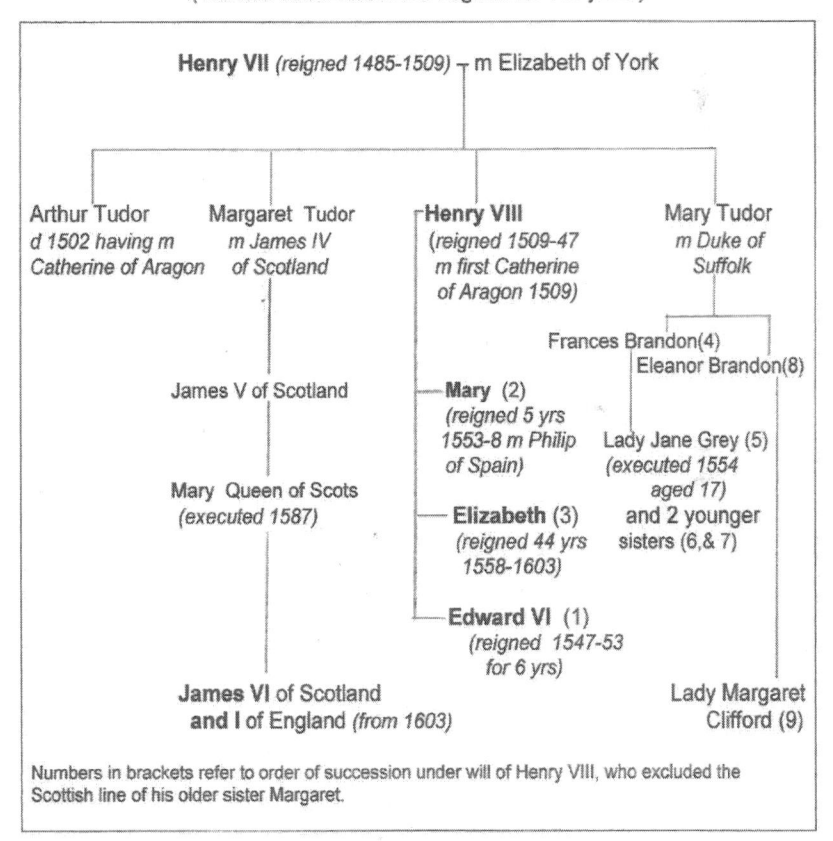

Henry VII *(reigned 1485-1509)* m Elizabeth of York

- Arthur Tudor, d 1502 having m Catherine of Aragon
- Margaret Tudor, m James IV of Scotland
  - James V of Scotland
    - Mary Queen of Scots (executed 1587)
      - James VI of Scotland and I of England *(from 1603)*
- **Henry VIII** *(reigned 1509-47 m first Catherine of Aragon 1509)*
  - **Mary** (2) *(reigned 5 yrs 1553-8 m Philip of Spain)*
  - **Elizabeth** (3) *(reigned 44 yrs 1558-1603)*
  - **Edward VI** (1) *(reigned 1547-53 for 6 yrs)*
- Mary Tudor, m Duke of Suffolk
  - Frances Brandon(4)
    - Lady Jane Grey (5) *(executed 1554 aged 17)* and 2 younger sisters (6,& 7)
  - Eleanor Brandon(8)
    - Lady Margaret Clifford (9)

Numbers in brackets refer to order of succession under will of Henry VIII, who excluded the Scottish line of his older sister Margaret.

once successfully sued to Henry VIII for Mary's life, at a time when she was particularly stubborn against the will of her father. Cranmer had stood against the wishes of the nobles to divide up the chancel lands among themselves – insisting that they should wait until Edward VI's majority, as these lands of right belonged to him. These same nobles were now rowing back to gain the favour of the new Queen. Cranmer was the last and most reluctant of the Council to sign the order in favour of Lady Jane Grey succeeding Edward on the throne – but he had signed. He was persuaded in the end by the command of the young king himself on his deathbed. Cranmer had few illusions as to what was to come.

The reformation of King Edward's day, says Neal, *was the undertaking of a few bishops and privy councillors to change the religion of a nation only by the supremacy of a minor (the king), without the consent of the people in Parliament; and under the eye of the heir who was a declared enemy of all their proceedings.* [13] The Church of England was partly reformed and greed and corruption were widespread among those nobles who supported the new teaching. The English Reformation had become tainted. This work was now to go into the fire of persecution to prove whether it would last.

Despite all the difficulties, much was achieved in the reign of Edward VI. Ryrie calls these six years *the hinge on which the C16th turned.* [14] The hope of Cranmer and his brother ministers was that the reformation in doctrine, teaching and preaching would later be followed by reform of organisation and practice.

Chapter 9

A narrow escape from burning

And he said unto me: My grace is sufficient for thee. For my strength is made perfect through weakness. Very glad therefore will I rejoice in my weakness, that the strength of Christ may dwell in me. Therefore am I content in infirmities, in rebukes, in necessities, in persecutions, in anguishes for Christ's sake: for when I am weak, then am I strong. (2 Corinthians 12 Blocks A and B)

Prisoner

During those first few days of confusion after the death of Edward VI, while matters hung in the balance, Mary had issued a proclamation to the men of Suffolk that she would not alter the religion and laws of the land as settled in the days of her brother. She had no intention of keeping that promise. Princess Mary had stood aloof from the Reformation and loyal to the religion of her mother Catherine of Aragon from her earliest days. Bishop Ridley visited her when in her locality in 1552, offering to preach before her, to which she replied:

The door of the parish church adjoining shall be open for you if you come, and ye may preach if you will, but neither I nor any of mine shall hear you.

Ridley: *Madam, I trust you will not refuse God's word.*

Mary: *I cannot tell what ye call God's word – that is not God's word now, That was God's word in my father's days'.*

Ridley: God's word is one at all times, but hath been better understood and practised in some ages than in other.

Mary: You dared not for your ears have avouched that for God's word in my father's days that ye now do; and as for your new books, I thank God I never read any of them, I never did nor ever will do. And after many bitter words against the form of religion now established, ... she concluded with these words: *My lord, for your gentleness to come and see me I thank you, but for your offering to preach before me, I thank you never a whit.*

Ridley, withdrawing and by invitation being sat down to eat in that place, having eaten broke out sadly: *Surely I have done amiss. For I have drunk in that place where God's word offered has been refused, whereas if I had remembered my duty, I ought to have departed immediately and to have shaken the dust of my shoes for a testimony against this house.* These words were by the said bishop spoken with such a vehemence, that some of the hearers afterward confessed their hair to stand upright on their heads. [1]

The question for Coverdale and the others at the forefront of the Reformation was now whether to flee into exile or to stand firm in the prospect of imprisonment and death: *Among all the residue of godly bishops displaced and degraded, Myles Coverdale ... was one of the first of whom enemies of the gospel made a most assured account that he, above all others, should be burnt.* [2]

His dilemma and that of the other bishops was neatly summed up by Bishop Ridley. *Therefore if thou, O man of God, do purpose to abide in this realm, prepare and arm thyself to die: for both by Antichrist's accustomable laws, there is no appearance or likelihood of any other thing, except thou wilt deny thy Master Christ, which is the loss at the last of both body and soul unto everlasting death.* Ridley then proceeded to counsel those who still had their liberty. *My counsel, I say therefore is this, to fly from the plague and get thee hence.... And Christ our Saviour saith in the Gospel, 'When they persecute you in one city, flee unto another'.* ³

Marshalsea Prison

Beyond this old wall is the site of the old Marshalsea Prison, closed in 1842. This sign is attached to a remnant of the prison wall. Charles Dickens, whose father had been imprisoned here for debt in 1824, used that experience as the Marshalsea setting for his novel Little Dorrit.

HISTORIC SOUTHWARK

Most of the Marian martyrs who were burned in London were held in either Marshalsea, the Fleet or Newgate prisons, all of them in grim conditions.

Some 800 of the Reformers took this advice and went into voluntary exile after Mary came to the throne. Ridley himself felt that as a shepherd and a pastor of the London flock, he could not flee. Two of his three prebendaries, Rogers and Bradford, also stayed to martyrdom. The third, Edmund Grindal, a future archbishop of Canterbury, went into exile. The Peace of Passau had been signed between the German Emperor and the Lutherans in 1552. While this was an interim measure, the permanent settlement being made at Augsburg in 1555, it gave toleration in those states and cities of Germany where the princes were Lutheran. The exiles went mostly to Emden, Wesel, Frankfurt and Strasburg in Germany; and Basle, Berne,

Zurich and Geneva in Switzerland where they received a sympathetic welcome.

Coverdale, now a prominent bishop, was a clear target for the new regime. Like most of the other bishops and leading preachers he chose to stay rather than flee. He was summoned to London to appear before the Privy Council with Bishop Hooper on 22nd August 1553 [3a] and remanded to *await their Lordes pleasures*. As yet the new regime had other matters to attend to. However, few were in any doubt as to what was in store. Peter Martyr, having packed his bags, left Oxford and returned to Strasburg. He wrote to his friend Bullinger on 3rd Nov 1553. *The most reverend the archbishop of Canterbury is imprisoned, and together with him are the bishops of Worcester* (Hooper*), Exeter* (Coverdale), *London* (Ridley)*, Latimer and several godly and learned preachers, for whom I earnestly entreat the abundant prayers of your church, forasmuch they are in the most extreme danger.* [4]

Gardiner and Bonner were quickly released from prison. Gardiner was made Lord Chancellor and Bishop of Winchester, and Bonner, Bishop of London. They, above others, were to be responsible for the religious policies of the new government. One of the Queen's first acts, on 18th August, was to issue a proclamation from her Council that none should preach or read openly the Bible in churches, or print any books without her Majesty's licence.

During this time Coverdale wrote a long letter to an Exeter friend, making clear his own resolution to live and die by his beliefs (Appendix 4). The letter concludes: *As for me, I have entered my account with the Lord my God, who of His mercy, I doubt not will make it up and graciously perform His promise. I have cast my pennyworth already, as evil a hearer as I am, what this will cost me being fully determined never to consent to unlawful things for any pleasures of life… Sure I am, though the flail of adversity beat never so hard, and the wind of affliction blow never so sore, it shall but break my straw and blow away my chaff; for the corn that the Lord hath appointed for His own barn shall be safe enough, and kept full well by the help of Him that is the owner thereof, to whom be all honour and praise.* [5]

One document of great importance did emerge from the prison, signed by twelve of the men who faced death. It was a simple statement of the grounds on which they would not submit to the Queen's will. It begins: *We are (in prison), not as rebels, traitors, seditious persons, thieves, or transgressors of any laws of this realm, but alone for conscience we have to God, and his most holy word and truth…. Some of us have been in prison 8-9 months without books or paper.* Then simply and clearly it states their beliefs on the matters in which they differed from their captors and for which the majority of them were soon to be burned at the stake:

1. *We believe all the canonical books of Old and New Testament to be the Word of God and written by inspiration of the Holy Ghost, and therefore to be heard as the judge of all controversies in matters of religion.*
2. *That the church, as the spouse of Christ, doth follow the doctrine of the Bible in all matters*
3. *We believe and confess concerning justification, that as it cometh only from God's mercy through Christ, so it is perceived and had by faith only: which faith is not an opinion, but a certain persuasion wrought by the Holy Ghost in the heart of man so as to submit to the will of God unfeignedly…. By this we disallow free will, works of merit and the necessity of auricular confession.*

> 4   The exterior service of God ought to be done in a tongue most to edify; and not in Latin, where the people understand not the same.
> 5   We confess and believe that God only by Jesus Christ is to be prayed unto and we disallow prayer to the saints departed this life.
> 6   We confess that as a man departeth this life, so shall he be judged at the last day, and is entered into the state of the blessed for ever or the damned for ever. We affirm purgatory and masses for the dead to be the doctrine of Antichrist
> 7   We confess and believe the sacraments of Christ, which be baptism and the Lord's supper, that they ought to be ministered according to the institution of Christ... And here we plainly confess, that the mutilation of the Lord's supper ... is antichristian. And so is the doctrine of transubstantiation....

At the end of the document is added: *To these things above do I, Miles Coverdale, late of Exon, consent and agree with these my afflicted brethren being prisoners (with mine own hand).* This suggests that Coverdale, while still waiting on the Council in London as he had been ordered to do, was not now as closely confined as his brethren. The document ends by stating that these men being obedient subjects would continue to pray for the government, and exhort all men to live peaceably towards the rulers. *But where they cannot obey but they must disobey God; there to submit themselves with all patience and humility to suffer as the higher powers shall adjudge; so are we ready to suffer, rather than consent to any doctrine contrary to that which we here confess.... The Lord of mercy endue us all with the Spirit of His truth and grace of perseverance therein unto the end. Amen.* [6] These men were under no illusions as to what was before them.

Queen Mary's Marriage

So Coverdale lay with his brethren during the year 1554 under restraint or in prison, awaiting the Queen's pleasure. She was busy during this time. Negotiations went on quickly for her to marry Philip of Spain, heir to Charles V, the Holy Roman Emperor. The benefits to Spain of such a match were clear. France would now face a further enemy on the north side, as well as Spain in the south. England with its resources would be absorbed into the Spanish treasury and would be reclaimed from heresy. Philip landed in England with a train of nobles and a few days later on 25th July 1554, was married to Mary, Queen of England by Bishop Gardiner in Winchester Cathedral. This was shortly followed by the return to England of Cardinal Pole as Papal nuncio, the Pope's official representative. The outlook for the little green shoots of the Reformed religion in England had never looked darker.

Parliament was dissolved on 15th January 1555, having repealed all the laws against the Pope's authority which had been passed in England since 1529. Absolution was pronounced in a public ceremony, by Cardinal Pole to the whole Parliament of England, and prayers were ordered for the Queen, King, and the unborn child, which the Queen announced she was expecting, that it might be well-favoured and witty (clever) and a male child. The child's education and upbringing were to be at King Philip's choice. Above all, the laws against heresy were revived. The burnings were about to begin.

Within two weeks a start was made in the trial and condemnation of the first few: Hooper, Rogers, Taylor and Saunders were all excommunicated and committed to the sheriffs for burning. These sentences were carried out with all four dying bravely between 4th and 9th February. Coverdale would have felt the loss of the first two particularly. Rogers had shared his first exile and translation work in Antwerp. Hooper was a fellow Reformation bishop in King Edward's days. They were to be followed into the fires by some 280 more over the next three years, both ministers and hearers.

In reading through Foxe's detailed accounts of the examinations of those Reformers, arrested and examined before Bishop Bonner and others, one is struck time and time again as to how detailed and exact the knowledge of Coverdale's Bibles and Tyndale's New Testaments was, even among the less educated. One example will suffice, that of 19-year old William Hunter, an apprentice. The start of his trouble was in reading a Bible he found in the Church – probably the Great Bible still chained there. He was soon challenged by a priest, Atwell. *What, meddles thou with the Bible?'* ... To whom William answered and said: *Father Atwell, I finding the Bible here when I came, read in it to my comfort.* To whom father Atwell said: *It was never a merry world since the Bible came abroad in English.* To which William answered saying, *Father Atwell, say not so, for it is God's book, out of which every one that hath grace may learn to know both what things please God, and also what displeaseth Him.* William Hunter, after a number of examinations was burnt at the stake several months later, for denying transubstantiation [7]

Coverdale was now in extreme danger. Why would he be treated differently from his brethren? His life was saved by the intervention of Christian III, King of Denmark, Norway and Iceland. During his second exile Coverdale had travelled to Denmark to visit his kinsman, Dr John MacAlpine, married to Coverdale's wife's sister. This minister, being the king's chaplain, prevailed with his sovereign to write a letter to Queen Mary on Coverdale's behalf.

The king wrote on 25th April 1554 in friendly and cordial terms, begging the Queen, as a favour to him, not to try Coverdale for heresy but to pardon and release him and allow him to be sent over to Denmark. [8]

Her Majesty, in reply, stated that Coverdale was not charged with heresy, but only for debt due to her treasury: that nevertheless she would look favourably on him for the sake of the King of Denmark. As she wished to maintain cordial relations between England and Denmark, so King Christian could be sure she would fall in with his request. However, for some months nothing was done, so that Coverdale's Danish friends began to fret as to her intention in the matter. So the King of Denmark wrote a second time to Queen Mary on Coverdale's behalf.

Christian III (1509-59) King of Denmark, Norway and Iceland

In this second letter, dated 24th September 1554, the king expressed his thankfulness that Coverdale's offence was merely a debt rather than heresy, and that relying on the merciful nature of Queen Mary, he had every confidence that she would fall in with his request. He assured the Queen again that it would increase the bonds of friendship between the two countries if she granted him this small favour. [8]

The outcome was that Queen Mary had little choice but to release Coverdale. She had stated he was only in prison for debt, and relations between the two countries were too important to allow the king to be rebuffed by refusing such a request. She delayed, but finding no other way of keeping Coverdale in her power, she grudgingly let him go some five months after King Christian's second letter   Her answer to the king was dated the 18th February, 1555.

In her letter, the Queen wrote: *And although he is our natural born subject, and is not yet freed from a debt of certain monies, which by law he was bound to pay to our treasury; yet we held that a greater weight was to be given to your request, than to our debt.* So Queen Mary sent Coverdale into his third exile. Her Council gave him a passport on 19th February 1555 to go to Denmark and take with him *two of his servants, his bagges and baggages, without any unlawfull let or searche.* [9] This entry suggests that Coverdale, like Hooper, had already sent his wife to her relatives abroad when he was committed to prison.

Why did the Queen release Coverdale who, as one of the five most prominent bishops and preachers on the Reformed side, she would have kept most eagerly and keenly in her power?   The answer is not difficult to deduce. Christian III, King of Denmark, Norway and Iceland had been present at the Diet of Worms in 1521, as one of the north German nobles in the train of the Emperor. Becoming a decided Lutheran, he had to dispute the throne of Denmark against the Roman Catholic nobility who wished to keep the country within the Papal fold. The civil war which followed resulted in complete victory for the king. Soon after, he had to fight a war against the Dutch, ruled as they were by Spanish king, Charles V. That war he had won by closing the Sound, the entrance to the Baltic. This denied Dutch merchants the lucrative trade with the Baltic ports, which was important to them.

As a result of his victories, the Lutheran church became the state church in his kingdoms of Denmark, Norway and Iceland, and the king an important ally of the northern German princes. Now in the mid-1550s, the Spanish King Charles, father-in-law to Mary, was waging a bitter war for supremacy against the other great European power, France. This war heaved to and fro, sometimes one side and sometimes the other gaining the upper hand. It was important to Spain to keep the northern German electors and nobles as well-disposed as possible during this time, especially in hopes that they might cause a distraction by stirring up trouble on the eastern borders of France. Also the resources of the Low Countries were needed. The Dutch bitterly resented the taxes levied on them to help finance the war, but could do little about it. The closure of the Baltic trade against them by the king of Denmark would have had a serious effect. Against these considerations, what was the life and liberty of one heretic? Coverdale was thus released to the Danish King. Of the leading evangelical bishops and ministers who were in prison, Coverdale was the only one whose life was spared honourably, without recanting.

Chapter 10

Third Exile. A wanderer

They went astray in the wilderness in an untrodden way, and found no city to dwell in. Hungry and thirsty, their soul fainted in them. So they cried unto the Lord in their trouble, and He delivered them from their distresses. He led them forth by the right way, that they might go to a city where they dwelt. (Ps 106 (now Ps 107) Block A)

Wanderings in Denmark and Germany

Coverdale first travelled to Denmark with his wife and two servants, to express his gratitude to the king for his intercession and to see his kinsfolk. It would have been a warm reunion between the two sisters, Agnes Macalpine and Elizabeth Coverdale, after eleven years of separation in peril and hardship. The University of Copenhagen gave him a present of wine and claret [1] and it is said that the king offered him a position in the Danish church. However, he refused. Mozley suggests that it was because of *his ignorance of the language. He was now sixty-seven years old, and felt he could employ his few remaining years more profitably in serving his afflicted brethren in Germany than in mastering a new tongue.* [2] However, there may well have been a more compelling reason: the Lutheran views on the Lord's Supper were by this time out of line with Coverdale's beliefs and those of his English brethren.

So he refused all offers of employment in Denmark, and left in the summer of 1555 for Wesel, a port on the river Rhine in northern Germany, close to the Dutch border. *After Richard Bertie and his wife the Duchess of Suffolk arrived safely in Wesel in Westphalia early in the Spring of 1555 the rumours of their presence soon brought many more English exiles to the town, when it pleased God also that Master Coverdale, after he had been with the King of Denmark, should also come to the same town.* [3] Here too came John Bodley, his Exeter friend, with his household. A threefold rebellion against Queen Mary, in Kent, the Midlands and Devon had been put down. Bodley was under suspicion, partly because of his known support of the Reformed cause but also on account of the Devon uprising.

While at Wesel Coverdale took up his pen again, as well as pastoring this flock of exiles. In 1549 he had translated one tract of the Zurich minister Werdmuller into English, and now produced three more. No doubt Coverdale's heart and affections were with his brethren in England who were now giving their lives for their beliefs. His motive may well have been to strengthen their resolve. The first tract: *A most fruitful, pithy and learned treatise how a Christian man ought to behave himself in danger of death*, had bound with it Lady Jane Grey's last letter to her sister, written the night before her execution.

The perils surrounding the exiles were driven home by the arrest of a number of the printers who had found ways to return with books into England. *Divers persons were taken and committed to sundry prisons for selling and having books sent into England by the preachers that had fled to Germany, so that within a fortnight little less than threescore were imprisoned for this matter.* [4]

Coverdale only stayed four months at Wesel, in the summer of 1555. From the letters of Thomas Lever, who was elected to replace Coverdale as pastor, we can glean that the magistrates at Wesel asked the English colony either to embrace Lutheran practices or to leave. Why was this?

Having tried in vain to subdue the Lutheran nobles in the years after the Augsburg Interim of 1548, when he tried to crush the Reformation in Germany, Charles V came to terms. The Peace of Augsburg signed in 1555 between the Emperor and the German Lutheran princes, just before Coverdale reached Wesel, was on the basis of 'whose realm, his religion'. This provided that the religion of the prince, either Lutheran or Roman Catholic, became the religion of the state and its inhabitants. This gave a legal basis for the Lutheran confession, but it did not recognise the teachings of Zwingli and Calvin.

Great respect was shown to Luther by the Swiss, who honoured him as the first instrument of the Reformation. However, the Germans, Luther at the fore, were unwilling to accept the Swiss as brethren. Some extremely intemperate articles flowed from Luther's pen against the Swiss – something which had deeply disturbed Coverdale during his second exile, when the dispute was still running with great heat. The result was the shutting out of the Swiss from the Peace of Augsburg. Article 17 of the Peace treaty stated quite plainly: *All such as do not belong to the two above named religions* (i.e. Lutheranism or Roman Catholicism) *shall not be included in the present peace, but shall be totally excluded from it.* The Lutheran princes had suffered in the wars waged against them by the Emperor during the previous decade, and were nervous of overbalancing this peace. On his side the Emperor had no interest whatever in giving liberty to the Reformed religion. Indeed, many of this persuasion were being hounded and burned in both the Low Countries and in Spain.

The practical result of all of these factors: the divisions on the Lord's Supper, the weakness of the negotiating position of the German nobles compared to the Emperor, Luther's intemperance and Calvin's teaching all contributed to the shutting out of the Swiss from the Peace of Augsburg. It would also have contributed to Coverdale's unease in Germany during his third exile, and his unwillingness to settle at either Wesel or Bergzabern for long.

Thomas Lever tells us what happened next at Wesel. *For since their late pastor* (Myles Coverdale) *had left them of his own accord, and the magistrates had forbidden them the use of the sacraments ... the English exiles left.* [5] This is clarified by a later letter from Lever: *And thus we English, driven from our own country by popery, and from Wesel by Lutheranism, are now, most of us, by our mutual wishes, counsels and assistance, tending to one spot, where it is still permitted us freely, sincerely and openly to acknowledge and worship Christ.* [6] That was Switzerland, where they were warmly welcomed in the cantons of Basle, Berne and above all Geneva, where the largest group eventually settled.

Back to Bergzabern

So why did Coverdale leave Wesel and the small group of exiles? His friend Conrad Herbert, hearing of his arrival in Germany, sent him a warm invitation to resume his work at Bergzabern where he had resided for five years in his second exile. *But although I have had an interview with him, the business itself is referred to the prince for his determination, on his arrival, which is looked for to-morrow. The issue of the affair, whatever it may be which God may grant to it, shall be announced to you by letter.* [7]

It is possible that Coverdale was intending, from the time of King Christian's intervention, to return to the Strasburg area where he was well known and respected, and where he and his family would enjoy comparative security. An entry in the Strasburg Council minutes for 30th July 1554, when Coverdale was still in England under restraint (but after the King of Denmark had first requested his release), states that Michael Angelus *would like to become a citizen but wishes to be excluded from bearing arms.* [8] This request was granted without hesitation by the Council, suggesting that unlike some Englishmen who made similar requests, the Council had complete confidence in Coverdale.

Coverdale was also conscious of the grave danger facing the Duchess of Suffolk and her household at Wesel, just over the border from the King of Spain's Dutch territories. Queen Mary and her husband, Philip of Spain, took a dim view of the nobility who tried to flee out of her reach and they were about to summon the Duchess back to England. Could he help them?

*It pleased God also that master Coverdale, after that he been with the King of Denmark, should come to the same town (*Wesel*): who preached there no long time, till he was sent for by Wolfgang, Duke of Bipont,* (otherwise known as Count of Zweibrucken) *to take the pastoral charge of Bergzabern, one of his towns in Germany. At whose coming to the Duke, he made it known, both to himself and to other noblemen about him, of Master Bertie and the Duchess being in the Low Countries. They (understanding the danger that might come unto them in those parts; as also calling to remembrance what great courtesy strangers had found in England at the Duchess's hands) made offer that, if they were forced to remove, or otherwise if it pleased them, they should have the Castle of Weinheim, by Heidelburg, within the liberties of Otto Henricus the Palsgrave, and a godly prince; who most gladly gave consent to the same.* [9]

There is a letter in the Lambeth Palace archives, dated 24th January 1556 from Christofel, Landschade of Steinach, to

Katherine Bertie, offering a house at Weinham *for the gospel's sake exiled out of England, as he is informed by Mr Michael, Englishman, pastor at Bergzabern* (Coverdale).[10] Evidently at Coverdale's intercession, the Castle of Weinheim was put at the disposal of the Duchess and her husband and retinue, safely within the lands of a devout Lutheran nobleman. One of Coverdale's letters makes clear he was actively helping the Duchess as well as moving his family to Bergzabern.

With regard to the business, concerning which you requested me to inquire relating to the most illustrious duchess of Suffolk, her very distinguished husband, whom I spoke to on this subject at Frankfort, assured me that her grace, as far as money was concerned, owed nothing at all either to our excellent father Bucer, or to any other persons. But when I shall return to Wesel, from whence I must now bring up my dear wife to this place, I will make a diligent examination into the whole business. [11]

That it was none too soon for the Duchess to remove herself to somewhere safer than Wesel we understand from a tip-off given her at this juncture by the English Ambassador to the Low Countries. He warned her that one of Philip's generals, with ten companies of soldiers, was about to pass through Wesel and capture the Duchess. Her danger was also demonstrated by the capture in the area of Sir Peter Carew (a prominent Devon nobleman who had led the rebellion in those parts against Queen Mary) and Sir John Cheke (former tutor to Edward VI), both of whom having also left England without permission, who were returned to an English prison. Early in 1556, one Brett was sent by Queen Mary to order the return of the Duchess. When he reached Weinheim Castle, on 10th July 1556, with his warrants, he tells us what happened.

When I came afore the castle gates, I found them fast shut, and a stripling, like an English lackey standing afore them. Of him I demanded if the said Duchess and Bertie were within. The said lackey answered me, yea, and scarcely had spoken this word, but one looking out of a grate in the gate, asked who I was and what I would have? I told him that I would gladly speak with the said Duchess and Bertie, and that I had letters to deliver them from certain their friends. He demanded me my name and I told him. Then he bade me tarry at the gate and he would go tell the Duchess of me. And with that he and a companion, went a speedy pace towards the inward parts of the castle. In the mean space while they came again, we without the gate might hear a noise of laying down stones in the window of a little turret over the gate and casting up our eyes, we saw one or two look out as though they were louth to be seen; which immediately after began to cry in French 'kill them, kill them', with this we heard also folks coming towards the gate. [12] Brett retreated at great speed as fast as his horse would take him! The Duchess and her household eventually removed to Poland until the end of Queen Mary's reign.

The hardship endured by the exiles was reflected in this letter by Coverdale's friend Thomas Lever. *For we English, after our banishment from England, our removal from Wesel, and wanderings over almost all Germany, have suffered a repulse in Basle, and are at length compelled to have recourse to the hospitality of the people of Berne. For the counsellors of King Ferdinand, will not allow any Englishmen who are exiles for the sake of religion, liberty of passage through that territory of Ferdinand which lies between Strasburg and Basle. Whence you may easily perceive the length, fatigue, expense, difficulty and danger of our journey, and how greatly we are in need of protection, advice, liberality and assistance.* [13]

There is a small glimpse of their poverty in Christine Garrett's research. *Even the richest of them could not buy accommodation in the crowded walled cities of the Rhine valley. They had literally to be herded together, sometimes five families to a house in quarters far too small for them. In John Kelke's house at Frankfurt, were five families numbering 22 persons. In the case of Thomas Saunders one roof sheltered only three families but 28 persons.* [14]

At last the little band of exiles from Wesel gained shelter within the canton of Berne. The Lords of Berne gave them a warm welcome, at the request of Thomas Lever and John Bodley, to settle in any town of the canton, to practise their religion and also the manufacture of English cloth. Berne itself had recently had a large influx of refugees from Italy, but space was found at Aarau, where seven houses were made available for the English refugees. Here a congregation of some 93 exiles found a home in August 1557. *M Lever and the company at length chose Aarau for their resting place, where the congregation lived together in godly quietness among themselves, with great favour of the people among whom for a time they were planted.* [15]

Miles Coverdale, his wife and two children went to reside with this group in the little town of Aarau. [16] The register of exiles at Aarau is the only known mention of his children, suggesting that they died young. It is likely he left Bergzabern, after a twenty-two month stay, for the same reason as he left Wesel: increasing difficulty in ministering to a Lutheran congregation and administering the Lord's Supper. He may too have had a wish to nurture his family in an English-speaking environment, or in the atmosphere of greater stability which Switzerland offered. We find him in second place, after the pastor Thomas Lever, on a list of householders in the congregation. This suggests that, with his amiable and homely disposition, it was relatively easy for Coverdale to settle under another man's pastoral care, though it was the flock of which he had been pastor but a short time previously. The Frauenkloster (house) at the foot of the Stadtskirche (street) of Aarau was recorded as the home of the Coverdale family.

Coverdale in Geneva

International Monument to the Reformation in the grounds of Geneva University, by kind permission of the University: (left to right) Farel, Calvin, Beza, Knox. Inscribed in Latin on either side 'After darkness, light'.

However, Coverdale did not stay long in Aarau, moving with his family 160 miles to Geneva in 1558, and was given leave to settle there on 24th October 1558, three weeks before Queen Mary died in England. Why did he go to Geneva? What influence did it have on him?

The Geneva to which the exiles were drawn in 1554-8 would have remained buried in obscurity but for one eminent fact: John Calvin had been resident there from 1536, apart from a three-year gap from 1538-41 when, expelled by the authorities of Geneva, he lived in Strasburg. After Calvin's return, for the twenty-four remaining years of his life, his influence turned Geneva into a centre of the Europe-wide

Reformation. Geneva was a small city state with a population of only five thousand in 1500. However, the fame of its education and the warm, hospitable shelter given to those fleeing oppression swelled the population greatly.

Calvin is on record as having asked the Council on 25th November 1555 for a church in which the English exiles could meet. The Council was pleased to grant Marie La Nove church, which the English shared with the Italian refugees, each using the building at different times. The English church included the household of Coverdale's friend John Bodley, the Exeter merchant. Bodley's company of eleven persons was registered with the English Church on 8th May 1557. Let his son Thomas, twelve years old at the time, speak for himself. *My father in the time of Queen Mary, being known to be an enemy to Popery, was so cruelly threatened and so narrowly observed by those that maliced his religion, that for the safeguard of himself and my mother, who was wholly affectioned as my father, he knew no way so secure as to fly into Germany, where after a while he found means to call over my mother with all his children and family, whom for a time he settled in Wesel.... And from thence we removed to Frankfurt, where was in like sort another English congregation. Howbeit, we made no long tarriance in either of those two towns, for my father had resolved to fix his abode in the city of Geneva, where as far as I remember, the English church consisted of some hundred persons.... There I remained two years or more until such time as our nation was advertised of the death of Queen Mary and succession of Elizabeth with the change of religion. This caused my father to hasten into England.* Thomas writes of being taught by Calvin, Beza and others. Thomas Bodley, at the age of 20, became a fellow of Merton College, Oxford and later in life set up the Bodleian Library.
[17] It was in Frankfurt that Bodley's sixth child Miles was born, so called no doubt in honour of his friend the Reformer.

It was into this community Coverdale was welcomed; the Church book is silent as to when he arrived.[18] In Livre des

Anglois, the register of the exiles in Geneva, he is twice mentioned: once when elected senior (elder) of the English congregation on 16th December 1558, and the other when acting as 'witness' to the baptism of Knox's son Eleazer on 29th November. Not until 14th August 1559 did he take leave of Geneva to return to England. [19]

There is little doubt that it was the desire to continue his great work of Bible translation that drew Coverdale to Geneva: *Where after some two or three years, the learned which were at Geneva, as Bishop Coverdale, Master Goodman, Master Gilby, Master Sampson, Dr Cole, and Master Whittingham and who else I cannot relate, did undertake the translation of the Geneva Bible.* [20] Since the Great Bible of 1539-40, twenty years had seen a great advance in scholarship. Erasmus and others had found more Greek manuscripts and had further refined their work. Led by William Whittingham, the small band of dedicated exiles worked night and day to refine and improve the English Bible. It seems clear that Coverdale was motivated to go to Geneva to lend his help in translating the fourth of the important early English Bibles: the Geneva Bible, especially as this was being funded by John Bodley.

The translation begun in 1557 was finished in April 1560. Most of the congregation of exiles left in January 1559, once it was plain that England would welcome them home again. Coverdale and Bodley stayed some six months after the bulk of the congregation left, suggesting that Coverdale's role was to use his vast experience to revise and correct, so that the Bible ready for the press. *The congregation prepared themselves to depart, saving certain which remained behind the rest to finish the Bible and the Psalms, both in metre and in prose, which were already begun at the charges of those who were of most ability.* [21] Coverdale's ear for and experience of the Psalms, both in prose and metre, would have been most welcome to the little band of translators.

Part of a page from the metrical Psalm 1 at the back of Geneva Bibles

The Psalms for singing were put into a large number of different metres, the concern being more for faithfulness to the Hebrew than musical effect. They were printed in the back of the Bibles, and their use became widespread in a fairly short time in England once the Elizabethan reign began. John Jewel, himself a Marian exile and now a bishop, writing in March 1560, had this to say: *As soon as they had once commenced singing in public, in only one little church in London, immediately not only the churches in the neighbourhood, but even the towns far distant, began to vie with each other in the same practice. You may now sometimes see at Paul's Cross after the sermon, 6,000 persons, young and old, of both sexes, all singing together and praising God.* [22] Enemies, and even the new Queen, spoke scornfully of 'Geneva jigs'.

The Geneva Bible reached heights of accuracy and scholarship not before seen in English versions. Not least, it was the first English version to divide chapters into verses, the first to have some editions in Roman print rather than Gothic, and was cheap and well printed. Besides the metrical psalms it had large numbers of marginal notes, pithy and clear, making it the Bible of choice throughout the Elizabethan years and beyond. It was the first English Bible to use italics with which to render the sense of words not specifically in the original but whose use was needed to convey the sense of the passage in English. Offence caused by the marginal notes among the rulers meant it was not printed in England until 1576 after the death of Archbishop Parker.

As a measure of its popularity, between 1560 when published and 1615, according to the Historical Catalogue of Printed Bibles, the Geneva Bible went through 91 editions, and sold about 500,000 copies. It was the Bible of the home and hearth and of the ordinary people, being both affordable and of a reasonable size to carry.

> 19 And the midwiues answered Pharaoh, Because the Ebrew 8 women *are* not as the women of Egypt: for they are liuely, and are deliuered yer the midwife come at them.
> 20 God therefore prospered the midwiues, and the people multiplied and were very mightie.
> 21 And because the midwiues feared God, therefore he ʰ made them houses.

g *Their disobedience herein was lawfull, but their dissembling euill.*
h *That is, God increased the families of the Israelites by their meanes.*

Geneva Bible Exodus 1.19-21. Marginal notes such as this one, stating that disobedience to rulers is, in some circumstances, lawful made the Geneva Bible unpopular with rulers.

By contrast, the Bishops Bible, the official version used in churches by authority of the Queen and clergy from 1568, went through eleven editions, reprints of the Great Bible five, and the Roman Catholic Douai Bible one edition. The Geneva was the Bible of the Scottish kirk, of Cromwell's soldiers and of the Pilgrim Fathers. *The Geneva Bible became enormously popular… It became the Bible of the Puritan faction in England and in the puritan diaspora on the Continent and in America.* [23] Even in a fourth generation, sixty years after the production of the King James version, it was widely used and consulted in both nonconformist England and among the American colonists. George Offer says of John Bunyan, whose ministry spanned from 1655 to his death in 1688: *It was his habit to consult the two translations then in common use. The present Authorized version, first published in 1611, is that to which he usually refers; comparing it with the favourite Puritan version made by the refugees at Geneva, and first printed in 1560. He sometimes quotes the Genevan, and so familiar were the two translations, that in several instances he mixes them in referring from memory to passages of holy writ.* [24] John Knox being pastor for a time over the little band of English exiles at Geneva, it is not surprising that these were the first Bibles printed in Scotland in 1575, and recommended by both kirk and Parliament.

Geneva Church given by Council for use by English exiles.

Influence of Geneva on Coverdale

What influence did Geneva have on Coverdale and the other returning refugees? While John Calvin wielded no secular power, his ministry first modelled Geneva into what John Knox described as *the most perfect school of Christ which has been seen on earth since the days of the apostles.* Calvin's pen and his lectures attracted students from all parts of Protestant Europe, and refugees arrived on a weekly basis from the hostile countries around. It is reckoned that the population of Geneva had reached 30,000 by his death. In addition, he corresponded with rulers and church leaders throughout Europe who favoured the Reformation, sending out ministers into all the surrounding countries. When a pastor was needed in 1564 for the French church in London Grindal, by now bishop of London, wrote to Calvin asking for a nominee.

It is likely that Coverdale and others were significantly influenced by Calvin and the church order he had instituted in Geneva. The first Geneva Bible of 1560 had a preface by Calvin as well as his catechism bound up with it. When Calvin was asked for his view of the 1552 English Prayer Book, his reply was uncompromising: *Nor do I see for what reason a church should be burdened with these frivolous and useless, ... pernicious ceremonies, when a pure and simple order of worship is within our power.* [25] The exiles had as their service book: *The form of Prayers and Administration of the Sacraments used by the English congregation at Geneva (approved by John Calvin 1556)*. This was a translation from Calvin's own service book.

When John Knox returned to Scotland to undertake the great task of leading the Scottish Reformation, he brought this Order of Service from Geneva almost without change. It was Calvin's teaching transposed into a nation, rather than into a city state. Knox, who had been united to the English exiles by common bonds of adversity, having returned to Scotland finally in May 1559, kept in close touch with his brethren in Geneva. In one letter to Anna Lock, who was still in Geneva at that time, he reported: *We do nothing but go about Jericho, blowing with trumpets as God giveth strength, hoping victory by his power alone. Jesus Christ is preached even in Edinburgh, and his blessed sacraments rightly ministered in all the congregations where the ministry is established.* [26] He asked her to show the letter to his brethren still residing at Geneva.

Knox was as forthright as Calvin in his view of the English Book of Common Prayer: *We ought not to justify with our presence such a mingle mangle as now is commanded in your churches; ... It is not the leaving off of the surplice, neither yet the removing of external monuments of idolatry, that purgeth the church from superstition; for peculiar services appointed for saints days, many Collects as they falsely call them, in remembrance of this or that saint as a means of calling upon God ... are in my spirit, no small portion of papistical superstition.* [27]

Once news of the changes in England reached the exiles in Geneva and the other cities of Germany and Switzerland, there was overwhelming thankfulness at the prospect of a return to England. It was clearly the hope of those at Geneva that the changes in the Church of England which had come to a halt at the death of King Edward would now be carried further forward. A letter written on 15th December 1558 by the leaders of the exile church at Geneva summarises these hopes, and the expectation that the exiles would unite in urging further change. It was signed by Coverdale, Knox, Bodley and eight others of the English Church at Geneva.

After that we heard, dearly beloved of the joyful tidings of God's favour and grace restored to us, by the preferment of the most virtuous and gracious Queen Elizabeth; we lifted up our hearts and voices to our heavenly Father: who hath not only by his due Providence nourished us in our banishment, preserved us and as it were carried us on his wings; but also heard our prayers, granted our requests, pitied our country, and restored his Word. So that the greatness of this marvellous benefit overcometh our judgments and thoughts, how to be able worthily to receive it, and to give thanks for the same....

And because all impediments and cavillations of adversaries might be removed; it seemed good to have your godly counsel and brotherly conference herein ... that we might all join hearts and hands together in this great work; wherein no doubt we shall find many adversaries and stays. Yet if we (whose sufferings and persecutions are certain signs of our sound doctrine) hold fast together, it is most certain that the enemies shall have less power; offences shall be sooner taken away; and religion best proceed and flourish....

Most earnestly desiring you that we may together reach and **practice the true knowledge of God's Word; which we have learned in this our banishment, and by God's merciful Providence seen in the best Reformed Churches**, *that (considering our negligence in times past; and God's punishment for the same) we may with zeal and diligence, endeavour to recompense it, that God in all our doings may be glorified; our consciences discharged; and the members of Jesus Christ relieved and comforted.* [28]

Friendly replies were received from both Frankfurt and Aarau. The reply from Frankfurt pointed out that some had departed already for England, but doubted not they would agree, subject to the will of the Queen. Coverdale took his leave of the Council at Geneva and of his friends there on 14th August 1559 to return to England.

Chapter 11

Last years. An early Puritan

But God forbid that I should rejoice, save only in the cross of our Lord Jesus Christ, whereby the world is crucified unto me, and I unto the world.   For in Christ Jesus neither circumcision availeth anything nor uncircumcision but a new creature.   And as many as walk according to this rule, peace and mercy be upon thee, and upon Israel of God. From henceforth let no man put me to business, for I bear in my body the marks of the Lord Jesus. Brethren, the grace of our Lord Jesus Christ be with your spirit, Amen. (Galatians ch 6 Block B).

Elizabethan Church settlement

It was nearly a year into the new reign before Coverdale returned to London from his labours in Geneva. That year was eventful.

The third of Henry VIII's children to sit on the throne barely escaped with her life during the reign of her half-sister. It is said that Latimer's constant prayer in prison was that she would be kept safe. Poisoned against Elizabeth from the start due to the displacement of her own mother by divorce after 24 years of marriage, Queen Mary kept a close eye on her sister.   Elizabeth was committed to the Tower at one stage and only escaped execution by keeping well away from public affairs, by having mass said in her own church and by living quietly and in seclusion. The quick-witted princess survived to reign in her own right for 44 years. Well might she say on returning to the Tower as was the custom at the start of a reign: *Some have fallen from being princes in this land to be prisoners in this place: I am raised from being prisoner in this place to be a princess in this land. That dejection was a work of God's justice; this advancement is a work of His mercy.* She was 25 years of age.

When she came to the throne on 17th November 1558, Elizabeth was immediately surrounded by difficulties. The Pope had pronounced her illegitimate, which made her a natural target for those hoping to restore England to Rome. When Elizabeth wrote to the Pope to inform him of her accession and to ask his advice about the possibility of an alliance with Spain, his reply made clear to her that she could not look to that quarter for any help. *Elizabeth* wrote the Pope, *being illegitimate, cannot ascend the throne without my consent.... Let her in the first place submit her claims to my decision.*

There was little doubt as to Elizabeth's inclination in religion. She was Anne Boleyn's daughter. The first twenty years of her life she had been reared a Protestant and had been close to her brother, sharing for a time his tutors in the household of Henry VIII's last wife, Katherine Parr. Her subjects, too, were alienated by the persecutions and wholesale burnings of Queen Mary's reign. England became Protestant again. Nevertheless, the dangers surrounding Elizabeth were very real. It was as if the pattern of the last reign would be repeated, and as Elizabeth had then been the focus of Reformed hopes against her sister's Catholicism, so Mary Queen of Scots (next in line to the throne) would now become the focus of Roman Catholic expectations. The difference was that Elizabeth's resources were scanty: *While Mary Queen of Scots could hope for the blessing of the Pope, and would have the resources of France behind her. Scotland would be her base, and only the ill-fortified town of Berwick stood between her and the Catholic north of England.* [1]

The Queen proceeded cautiously. The exchequer was bare, harvests had been bad, there were widespread epidemics and heavy mortality; the State was in debt, and engaged in a disastrous war with France, having earlier in the year, in the dying days of Mary's reign, lost Calais England's last toehold in mainland France. Allies she had none who could be of help. Most of the bishops and councillors were still in place from the last reign. At the opening of her first Parliament, Lord Bacon spoke of *the great decay and losses of honour, strength and the peril that happened to this imperial crown of late time.... The marvellous waste of revenue of the crown, the inestimable consumption of the treasure, the exceeding loss of munition and artillery, incredible sums of money owing at that present time, the biting interest that was to be answered for.* [2]

At this point the needs of the Protestant nobles of Scotland, who with the encouragement of John Knox had declared for the Reformation, met the interests of Elizabeth to establish and stabilise her own throne. The Queen Regent in Scotland called for the help of French soldiers to subjugate her Protestant subjects. Elizabeth and William Cecil, her chief minister, were determined to have a stable, pro-English Protestant government north of the border if it were possible. So to the repeated requests of the Scottish nobles for help, she sent unofficially, in December 1559, Admiral Winter to blockade the French around St Andrews and Edinburgh. Meanwhile the French reinforcements being sent to Scotland in the same month were smashed up by a violent storm off the Dutch coast. The Treaty of Berwick followed, signed with the Scottish nobles, which pledged Elizabeth's help to maintain the liberties and freedoms of Scotland. One month later the English army entered Scotland with the aim of expelling the French. On 6th July 1560, the Regent having died while being besieged in the town of Leith where she and her French soldiers were bottled up by the English army, the Treaty of Edinburgh was signed. This notable day saw the triumph of Protestantism in Scotland as well as England, although in both nations there were many perils ahead. The French troops were to leave immediately, transported in English ships, and government in Scotland to be transferred to a Council of nobles. Within a few weeks, the Scottish Parliament had made Protestantism the religion of the state and declared the mass illegal.

Edinburgh statue of John Knox

Meanwhile, in England, both Reformed and Roman Catholic parties were beginning to stir, the one in hope and the other in alarm. The pulpits began to resound with the voice of controversy. Images began to be pulled down. The Queen gave order to the Lord Mayor of London in December 1558 that all preaching should cease, except the reading of the Bible and the litany in English until Parliament had met. Parker, Bill, and returning exiles Grindal, Cox, Whitehead and Pilkington with others, were called together to revise the 1552 Prayer Book. The forty-two church articles were slightly modified, reducing the number to thirty-nine. The government of the Church of England reverted to that of Henry VIII and Edward VI, except the Queen called herself Supreme Governor rather than Supreme Head. Key appointments went to Protestants of the 'Cambridge' type: those who had kept their heads down and quietly conformed in the last reign. Her chief advisers, William Cecil and Francis Bacon were of this type of reluctant conformist, as was her new Archbishop of Canterbury, Matthew Parker. More than any other of the Tudors, the Queen tried to make the Church as broad and comprehensive as possible, and one to which most of her subjects could subscribe. The Act of Supremacy, passed on 29th April 1559, required all ministers of the church, judges, councillors, and any who took the Queen's wages, to testify and declare *the queen's highness is the only supreme governor of this realm, as well in spiritual and ecclesiastical causes as temporal: and that no foreign prince or potentate hath or ought to have any power or superiority in this realm. And to promise to bear faith and true allegiance to the queen.* [3] This Act forbade any appeal to Rome, and also set up the Court of High Commission to deal with 'schism and heresy'.

Only some 170 clergy out of 9,400 refused the oath of supremacy. Fourteen of these were Roman Catholic bishops, which permitted complete change at the top of the Church of England. These bishops, to Elizabeth's credit, were allowed to depart in peace, although Bonner of London, White of Winchester and Watson of Lincoln, the most guilty of the blood of the Reformers in the last reign, were committed to prison, in the case of Bonner for the remaining ten years of his life. The Queen's attitude to these men was summed up in a letter she wrote: *Let us not follow our sister's example, but rather show that our reformation tendeth to peace and not to cruelty.* [4] Indeed, throughout her reign she tried to accommodate within her church those who still looked to Rome, except where she felt the stability of the throne was endangered. Some points the Queen felt might be offensive to her Roman Catholic subjects were struck out of the Book of Common Prayer, such as *from the tyrannies of the church of Rome and his detestable enormities good Lord deliver us.* The old festivals and the kneeling at communion were restored, as was the use of vestments by the clergy, all of which had been removed from the 1552 Prayer Book. Parliament passed quickly into law that no one should be punished for exercising religion as established in the last year of King Edward. The Act of Uniformity gave the Queen power to *ordain, and publish such ceremonies or rites as may be most for the advance of God's glory and for the edifying of the church.* She was also given the power to choose bishops. The Church of England thus owed its existence to the monarch, who appointed bishops, convened and dissolved its convocations and was the last court of appeal in matters of dispute. The Queen determined to steer a middle way, kept a crucifix in her chapel, and when Edwin Sandys, the new bishop of Worcester, reproved her she threatened to deprive him of his office!

Coverdale's return

Into this unsettled scene came the returning exiles from Germany and Switzerland. Many of them had sat at the feet of the great doctors of Geneva, Zurich, Basle and Strasburg and become accustomed to a simpler form of worship. The largest number came from Geneva and had used Calvin's Service book. *They came home threadbare, bringing nothing with them but much experience and learning.* [5] They were advised by the continental divines to thoroughly purge the Church of England. Their dilemma, however, was that if they insisted on the reforms which they had seen in the churches on the continent, they would be seen to destabilise the throne which was still on a shaky foundation.

It may be that if Grindal, Horn, Jewel, Parkhurst and Pilkington, exiles who soon became bishops, had stood firm at the first, it might have removed the grievances which afterwards caused division and separation between Anglicans and Puritans. Edmund Grindal, soon appointed bishop of London, wrote to Bullinger of their dilemma. *On our first return, and before we entered on our ministry, we contended earnestly for the removal of those things which have occasioned our present disputes; but we were unable to prevail, either with the Queen or with Parliament. We judged it best not to desert our charges for a few ceremonies, especially since the pure doctrines of the gospel remained in all their integrity and freedom.* [6]

This represented the view of the large majority. It is estimated that *for every returning exile who remained on the periphery, there were perhaps five who were offered and accepted preferment.* [7] There were four important reasons for this:

1) The slender and brittle thread by which Protestantism hung. *Elizabeth's first bishops were persuaded to accept unpalatable religious practices because they were convinced that the Queen alone could secure the Reformation in England.* [8] There was little point, they maintained, in dividing over church structure and ceremonies if it destabilised the throne. Much has been made of the Queen's ability to balance Puritan against Roman Catholic. However, this thesis does little justice to the loyal support the Puritans gave to the throne, even when their loyalty was not reciprocated!

2) The English church lacked preachers. If the Puritans refused office then the pulpits would either be shut or handed over to those who opposed them. The advice they were given from Zurich by their friends and mentors, pastors Bullinger and Gaultier, reflected this concern. One who was to be consecrated as a bishop wrote to Peter Martyr, then at Zurich, of his scruples. They included a) the use of caps and gowns similar to those used by the clergy in the

last reign who celebrated mass   b) the spoiling of church revenues by the nobles   c) kneeling at communion and the use of wafer bread   d) the processions associated with festivals which were still kept up   e) the crucifix on the communion table   f) the retention of such terms as *priest* and *absolution*. In Martyr's reply, he counselled his friend to accept office: *Because of the great need of ministers; whence if he and others declined to take ecclesiastical offices on them, they would give way to wolves and antichrists.* [9]

3) The doctrinal articles of the Church of England were little different from those of Geneva or Zurich.

4) The memory of the martyrs, many of whom were bound in ties of brotherhood to the returning exiles, left a savour. It was but two or three years since Cranmer, Ridley, Bradford, Hooper, Latimer, Rogers and many other members of the Church of England had stood firm in the face of a painful death.   Respect for their memory influenced many to conform to the church which the martyrs had founded and so recently led.

Coverdale was back in London in the Autumn of 1559, almost a year after Elizabeth I came to the throne. There is little doubt his bishopric of Exeter was reserved for him, left vacant until June 1560, and being one of the last to be filled. Hooker, by now MP for Exeter, informs us that *on the return of Mr Coverdale to England, I was one who advised him not to take up the bishopric of Exeter again.*[10]   This coincided with Coverdale's own views.   So he became a simple itinerant preacher.   He was not to lack employment.

Coverdale first preached at Paul's Cross, the most important preaching station in London, on 12th November 1559, and on a number of subsequent occasions until 1566.   When Matthew Parker was ordained Archbishop of Canterbury, in December 1559, Coverdale was drafted in to take part in the ceremony.   Unlike at his own ordination as a bishop in

1552, and unlike the other bishops in attendance, he was dressed in a simple black 'Geneva' gown.

At his first return to London,, Coverdale resided in the household of the Dowager Duchess of Suffolk, newly returned from Poland. A great support to the ministers who opposed the Elizabethan settlement, she wrote to William Cecil before her return of *the evils of halting between two opinions' in matters of religion, exhorting him to forward the true faith'.* [11] She, with her household, lived in the Minories, a series of houses around the church of that name. In a letter to William Cole in February 1560, Coverdale wrote: *My manner of life is still the same as when I left Geneva, except that I and my family are being entertained by the illustrious Duchess of Suffolk, who, like us, greatly abhors the ceremonies.* [11a]

Here Coverdale acted as governor to her children and chaplain to her household which numbered some eighty persons. *We find him being repaid the cost of Sir Thomas Elyot's dictionary, four copies of Lily's grammar, four copies of Aesop's fables and other school books.* [12] The normal practice of the Duchess was to spend the summer months at Grimsthorpe Castle, on her Lincolnshire estate, residing in the winter in London and attending the court. There is little evidence that Coverdale travelled to Lincolnshire. The Duchess herself stayed in London during the summer of 1562, where she caught smallpox, as did the Queen.

Lectureship. Catches the plague

This was the beginning of the age of Puritan lectureships, where the nonconformists could minister to a flock as a lecturer rather than as a regularly inducted Anglican clergyman. It freed them from the constraints of the Book of Common Prayer and other matters to which they objected. In 1563 Coverdale obtained a lectureship. It was a salaried post which he retained for the rest of his life. In the Court Books of the Clothworkers' Company, the following is recorded: *22nd November 1563. Divinity*

Lectures. At this court Mr Coverdale came and made request to have the goodwill of the Master, Wardens and Assistants, to have the reading of the Divinity Lecture at Whittington College, which request was to him granted upon condition that he may be admitted and do in all things the dead's will. [13] The will in question was that of one James Finch, who had set up the lectureship many years before this time.

Church of St Michael Paternoster Royal in the City of London [12]

The lectures were expositions on the Scriptures, given on certain weekday mornings at the parish church of St Michael Paternoster Royal and Coverdale was paid £10 per year, in quarterly instalments, for his work. The last instalment was paid to his widow a few days after his death, suggesting he had kept up the lectures to the end.[14] This church, in the City of London, had a considerable Puritan following. Not least of the local residents and worshippers at the church were John Bodley and his family, now returned and settled in London.   This might explain why Coverdale was appointed to the lectureship. Other former Genevan exiles also worshipped at the church. No doubt many flocked to the lectures. As the only noted bishop who had honourably survived the burnings, 'Father Coverdale' was by now greatly respected.

From time to time there were outbreaks of the plague in London, and in the severe attack of 1562 Coverdale caught it but, wonderfully, despite his old age and frailty, recovered to live for more than five further years.   London was a crowded city whose population had reached some 100,000 people, with many back lanes and narrow streets.   Coal from Newcastle and wood burned in the houses, often combined with the local fogs and damps characteristic of the low-lying site next to the river, caused unhealthy smogs. When, in addition to this, there was lack of drainage and sanitation, it became a fertile breeding ground for disease.

So great were the sufferings that a public letter was written by the clergy of London (ascribed to Coverdale's friend John Foxe but which Coverdale would have heartily endorsed) to the merchants and nobility. *Wherefore, being necessarily constrained by the pitiful cry and exclamation of the poor people of Christ here left in London, we are forced to write unto you speaking for them that cannot help themselves, that you of your clemency and Christian duty, will bestow some comfort upon your fellow members and poor brethren miserably here oppressed and consumed as well with penury as with pestilence, of which two, the one is in the hand of God only to stop, the other partly, under God in your hand to relieve.   Extend therefore we beseech you your helping hand, and in case you will not dare to visit them with your presence, yet visit them with your purses, that the Lord who peradventure doeth this to try you what you will do, may say to you: 'I was sick and you visited me.* [15]

Letters of the Martyrs

Coverdale's last publication was his *Letters of the Martyrs*, a collection of 224 letters, giving us an invaluable insight into the sufferings of the Marian prisoners, which he collected and published in 1564. Coverdale wrote a most tender preface. These had been his *familiar and acquainted* friends for many years, in some cases since his Cambridge days 40 years earlier: *Great cause have we to praise God: ... what heavenly strength and rich possession of constant faith, of ardent zeal, of quiet patience, of peace and joy in the Holy Ghost, he useth to arm them ... but also to join with them ourselves; in such sort that, looking to Jesus our captain, abiding the cross and despising the shame, as they did for the joy that was set before them, [we] may with much quietness of a good conscience end this our short course, to his glory, to the edifying of his church, to the confusion of Satan, to the hindrance of all false doctrine, and to our own eternal comfort in the same our Lord and alone Saviour Jesus Christ.* [16] Seventy-three of the letters published in his book were written by John Bradford and thirty-two by Nicholas Ridley.

Coverdale included twelve letters of John Philpott. Of Philpott he says: *They were held in various prisons, often in appalling conditions of privation and squalor, sometimes lying in fetters and chains. Despite such obstacles, many of the prisoners contrived to have ink, pens and paper. Under the guise of food, a bladder of ink powder was smuggled in to Philpot. When the keeper of the Bishop of London's coal house confiscated a pen-case and inkhorn from him, Philpot managed to find replacements.* [17]

Foxe published his first English edition of the Book of Martyrs in 1563. On his return to England from exile he travelled far and wide, checking his facts, adding new items as they came to light, and taking out anything which he could not verify. A large number of letters from the Coverdale volume are found in the second enlarged English edition of Foxe's work, published in 1570.

The Bishop of London, Edmund Grindal, who had himself been in exile and knew Coverdale's worth, now suggested to Secretary Cecil that Coverdale could perhaps be considered for the bishopric of Llandaff in South Wales. *For if any competency of living might be made of it, I would wish it to Father Coverdale, now lately recovered from the plague. Surely it is not well that he who was in Christ before us all should be now in his age without stay of living. I cannot excuse us bishops herein, though I have somewhat to say for myself, for I have offered him divers things which he thought not meet for him.* [18]

There is little doubt that Coverdale refused the bishopric given his state of health and his Puritan disagreement over vestments. However, Bishop Grindal now found a way forward by appointing Coverdale as rector of St Magnus Church by London Bridge. Coverdale felt able to accept so long as he could quietly continue the practices as in Geneva. He wrote to Bullinger during this time: *As many of us as have cast out these things from the churches committed to our trust, cannot restore them without grievous offence and abominable impiety.* [19] The letter refers in particular to the vestments, the use of unleavened bread in the communion and receiving it kneeling.

The same issue as with his appointment as Bishop of Exeter cropped up again in that Coverdale was too poor to pay the first fruits, in this case £60 (the payment in advance to the Crown of the first year's income). Consequently, we have letters from him to Archbishop Parker, to Sir William Cecil and to the Earl of Leicester, asking them to intercede with the Queen to waive the payment. His letter to Sir William Cecil gives us a glimpse of the hardship he had endured since his imprisonment: *That whereas my lord of London, tendering as well mine age as my simple labours in the Lord's harvest, hath very gently offered me the pastoral office and benefice of St Magnus in London; even so it may please your honour to be means for me to the queen's most excellent majesty, that in favourable consideration, not only how destitute I have been ever sith my bishoprick was taken from me, and that I never had pension, annuity, or stipend of it these ten years and upward; but also how unable I am, either to pay the first-fruits.* [20]   The favour was speedily granted by the Queen at the request of her favourite, Robert Dudley, Earl of Leicester, who sent a message to Coverdale to this effect.

St Magnus Church, London Bridge, as rebuilt after the Great Fire of London

The next known record of him is performing a duty on behalf of the University of Cambridge. Bishop Edmund Grindal in his high office should also have been a Doctor of Divinity, but owing to the interrupted nature of his studies this had not happened. The Vice-Chancellor of the University appointed

Coverdale to perform the ceremony. This was done at the Bishop of London's residence at Fulham Palace. The oath of loyalty to the Queen on this occasion was administered by Coverdale's former lawyer assistant at Exeter, Dr Robert Weston, who by this time was Commissioner for Oaths in London.

First attempt to make the Puritans conform 1564-6

Coverdale was to keep his post as Rector of St Magnus Church for just two years. Much of the struggle which now ensued between Queen and Puritans was confined to the province of Canterbury. In much of Wales and northern England, many of the clergy had conformed to the Elizabethan settlement in the same way as they had to Mary's: *After the said change made by Queen Elizabeth, the greatest part even of those who ... had been Catholics, did not well discern any great fault, novelty or difference from the former religion save only in the choice of language, in the which difference they conceived nothing of substance or essence. And so easily digested the new religion and accommodated themselves hereto; especially in Wales and other like places remote from London.* [21] As Elizabeth was more concerned with political loyalty than religious zeal this may not have concerned her greatly. This was also true in the north of England. In an interesting account of the ministerial labours of Bernard Gilpin of County Durham, we are told that: *this barbarous people were excluded from all means of better information ... that in that part of the kingdom, through the designed neglect of bishops and justices of the peace, king Edward's proclamation for a change of worship had not even been heard of at the time of that prince's death.* [22]

In and around London, matters were different. Many of the bishops shared a desire to see greater Reformation of the Church and had to this point turned a blind eye to the more Genevan practices of their brethren. But when the Queen made an occasional intervention demanding conformity, the bishops by their vow of obedience were bound to execute her wishes.

One such occurred in 1565, when it was ordered by the Queen in her letter of 25th January to Parker, Archbishop of Canterbury, that he treat nonconformity with great severity. *Both in ecclesiastical and civil polity, by public officers and ministers following… one rule, form and manner of order … without diversities of opinions, or novelty of rites and manners…. She, considering the authority given her of God … meant not any longer to suffer these evils thus to proceed, spread and increase in her realm.* [23] The result was that on 3rd March, six of the ministers were summoned to appear before a Commission of Archbishop Parker and four bishops to confer and to explain their nonconformity. In a coordinated effort to persuade the bishops to tolerate Genevan practices, Coverdale and another nineteen leading ministers wrote on 20th March *in a very elegant but submissive style*, requesting their forbearance in these matters. Coverdale's was the first signature. Seventeen of the twenty were returned exiles. [24]

That their reasons for this address were many and great, vis that conscience was a tender thing, that ought not to be touched or angered…. That their conscience told them, that, if they should recollect to their memories former times, God and Christ, and the faith of the primitive Church would be on their side. The Jewish kings, by God's command, abolished all the vessels instruments and furniture of idolatry. Christ rejected all the leaven, fasts, washings, phylacteries, and fringes of the Pharisees…. That they, the Bishops themselves, if they might have leave to appeal to their own consciences, were of the same opinion with them, and that they could wish all these stones of offence were removed. Lastly they appeal to the purer churches of Germany, France and Scotland; in which religion is not only preserved unstained, but such rites are observed as are simple and undefiled testimonies and signs of religion, taken from Christian churches not borrowed from Roman synagogues. In fine, that they themselves were not ignorant what a great scandal would arise hence: that the adversaries would insult over them in their afflictions, and would ... be still more pleased with their own inventions, after they should see it not only retained by them but by them obtruded on their brethren.

Of some encouragement to Coverdale and others to stand firm was the way that their brother exile, John Knox, had remarkably triumphed in Scotland in establishing the worship as he had known it in Geneva. As Thomas Randolph, the English agent in Scotland, ruefully wrote to Cecil: *Mr Knox ... upon Sunday last, gave the cross and the candle such a swipe, that as wise and learned as himself wished him to have held his peace.* [25]

Matters came to a head in March 1566, when Archbishop Parker, with Grindal in attendance, called before him 110 pastors and curates of London, and required them to wear the priestly garments. They were not permitted to speak, only to answer yes or no after their name. 61 subscribed, 37 did not and were suspended, some later to be deprived. Coverdale, although summoned with the others, absented himself, because of his health *and for other reasons*.

In July, he and two other ministers wrote to some of the Swiss ministers, making clear that they did not feel able to yield to the demands made on them by the bishops. The letter starts with a number of grievances: *An unleavened cake must be used (for the Lord's Supper), communion must be received by the people on bended knees, that out of doors must be worn the square cap, bands, a long gown and tippet; the white surplice and cope are to be retained in Divine service, ... and since a door would be opened to other mysteries of iniquity, and the love of the godly be offended, and the pride and boldness of the wicked be encouraged, without even any pretence of edification ...* **we consider it more for the good of the church to stand fast in our liberty than to depart** *... to the scandal of many and* *the downfall of pure doctrine.* [26] The bishops standing firm against their repeated pleas, within a few weeks Coverdale had resigned his living as rector of St Magnus Church.

The Puritans were in a hard place. If they refused the orders of the Queen, bishops and High Commission about the vestments and other matters they would be deprived. Yet the number of ministers was very few. This might cause the Reformation to go backwards rather than forwards. However, if they consented it would be against conscience. The Commission felt that by dealing harshly with them it would discourage others from resistance. A few remained resolute. When John Foxe was called before the Archbishop and asked to subscribe, he took his Greek New Testament from his pocket and said: *to this will I subscribe.* Many churches in London were shut up through lack of ministers, and the hands of the Reformers thereby weakened.

The bishops, to shore up their authority, wrote to Beza and Bullinger, who had given the exiles such kindly hospitality for the years of the Marian exile. Grindal published the conciliatory reply, rather hoping that it would strengthen his position and influence the exiles to fall in with the Queen's wishes. Coverdale received a letter from Bullinger shortly after apologising if a letter he had written to the bishops had increased Coverdale's difficulties. Bullinger states in the letter that he was not aware of the extent of the differences, expressing the hope that *faithful ministers will not be persecuted, and that the church of England be again purified from those things which are foreign to the purity of true religion.* [27]

Some of the ministers went to Scotland or overseas, some retreated to university posts, some became chaplains to noblemen. Coverdale kept his lectureship and preached occasionally as invited in different churches in London. Archbishop Parker was reminded by Sir William Cecil that churches lacked ministers, and the people were hungry for want of bread. In reply the Archbishop said that *when the queen put him upon what he had done, he told her that these precise folks would offer their goods and bodies to prison, rather than relent: and her highness had willed him to imprison them. He confessed that there were many parishes unserved; that he underwent many hard speeches, and much resistance from the people; but nothing more was to be expected.* [28] He also complained about the lack of cooperation he had from the Bishop of London. However, Grindal, who had himself been in exile, sympathised with the Puritans, and having more concern to promote good preaching would not push matters any further than he was forced to. He quietly restored some of the suspended ministers once the fuss had died down. As both sides now began to rush into print, the Privy Council forbade the printing of books against the Queen's injunctions.

In December 1566, after they had been deprived, a letter demonstrating full sympathy with the Puritans, signed by ten Scottish ministers, was sent by the General Assembly of the Church of Scotland to the Church of England bishops. Nineteenth century historian Lorimer argues persuasively that the letter was written by John Knox, but that he refrained from signing it. Elizabeth I was still hostile to Knox for a variety of reasons: his foremost offence in her eyes was the *First Blast of the Trumpet against the Monstrous Regiment of Women*, written against Queen Mary of England and Mary of Guise, Queen Regent of Scotland six years earlier. He had also clashed at Frankfurt in 1557, over the Book of Common Prayer, with some who were now bishops. Perhaps he felt the letter would convey more authority and less hostility if it came from the Church of Scotland speaking collectively. The letter, though, clearly displays Knox's forthright style: *We think ye should boldly oppose yourselves not only to all that power that will or does extol itself against God, but also against all such as does burden the consciences of the faithful farther than God hath burdened them by His own Word.* [29]

At last, in 1566, the ministers and people being at a loss to know what to do, and seeing the government and bishops were unwilling to relent, after much debate, at least one group in London came to a decision to separate from the Church of England. Their ministers were banished from the churches. There had been a separate underground congregation in London during the reign of Mary, so why not again? They were also encouraged by reports of the English congregation at Geneva, which had used an order and discipline *more in keeping with the Scriptures than the English service book*, and felt that it was, at this point in time, their duty to meet in private houses and elsewhere to worship God in a manner which would not offend their consciences. They would use the Geneva service-book. *Here was the era of separation, whereby people of the same country, of the same religion, and of the same judgment in doctrine, parted communions; one part being obliged to go aside into secret houses and chambers to serve God by themselves, which begat strangeness between neighbours, Christians and Protestants.* [30]

From this point on, for the likes of Coverdale, there was still much preaching activity in London – but there was an uneasy relationship with the authorities. Some were able to keep their positions within the church, and increasingly they kept lectureships in the churches or preached in private households. After March 1566 Coverdale and others who took the same position were not invited to preach at Paul's Cross again.

We gain a small window into this underground church which began meeting in 1566, when one hundred of the separatists were arrested at Plumbers Hall as they gathered for worship. In June 1567 they were examined before Grindal. Some of them were committed to prison, and were not released until 1569. One bold man named John Smith, in his examination, spoke of Coverdale as one of the few ministers they were willing to hear:

We had not separated from the parish churches, or assembled in private houses, so long as there was preaching and the administration of the sacraments without idolatrous gear. But when it came to it that all our preachers were displaced by your law, and we were troubled and commanded from your courts from day to day, then we bethought us of that congregation there was of us in Queen Mary's day, and of that congregation of Geneva ... therefore we revived the privy (secret) church using the Genevan order, the more so because we could hear none of the preachers in any parish church for the space of six or seven weeks together except Father Coverdale, of whom we have a good opinion, and yet (God knoweth), the man was so fearful that he durst not be known unto us where he preached, though we sought it at his house. [31]

Last days and death

As his strength failed Coverdale was increasingly a hearer rather than a preacher. This was for two reasons. First, he was increasingly frail. He had told Archbishop Parker in 1564 of his *weak and feeble age*, and that he *was not likely to live a year* [32] and in 1566 in a further letter to Parker: *I am unwieldy, and could well neither travel by land, nor altogether safely by boat.* However, as his failing strength permitted, he did preach in the church of Holy Trinity, the Minories. Coverdale is recorded as having preached nine sermons in this church in December 1567. Katherine, Dowager Duchess of Suffolk, was residing in the precincts, when in town, after her return from exile. From the entries in the registers and vestry books we find: *a servant of hers was buried there in that year, and her brother-in-law Mr Thomas Bertie, the year following.* [33] Importantly, the church had exemption from the authority of the Bishop of London at this time, which meant the parishioners had control of who to invite into the pulpit. *The Minories ... was the original home of puritanism in the sense that it seems to have been with the 'godly' who frequented its parish church that the name was first associated.* [34]

From 31st January 1568, Coverdale lived in a house belonging to the Merchant Taylors' company, in the parish of St Benet Fink, in Broad Street ward. The merchant Richard Hilles, a friend from his second exile, had been a freeman of the Merchant Taylors' Company since 1535, and was elected Master in 1561 (helping to set up Merchant Taylors' School with a £500 donation in that year). He had helped the destitute refugees during his stay at Strasburg from 1540-48 and was well known to Coverdale. He would have been pleased to provide a home for Coverdale and his second wife in his increasing weakness and frailty. Coverdale preached less in the last year of his life.

However, we do have a record of his last sermon, which Mozley states was preached at St Magnus Church, where he had been rector. *It happened that on a certain time that the whole parishioners being upon the knolling of the bell come to sermon, the preacher was not come. Whereupon certain men of the parish came unto him* (Coverdale) *and earnestly entreated that considering the multitude was great, and it was a pity they should be disappointed of their expectation, that it would please him to take the place for that time. But he excused his age and the infirmities thereof, and that his memory failed him, his voice scarce to be heard, and he was not able to do it, that they would hold him excused. Nevertheless such were their importunate requests that ... he did yield unto their requests; and between two men he was carried up into the pulpit, where God did with his Spirit so strengthen him, that he made his last and the best and most godly sermon he ever did in his life.* [35] This sermon was preached on 23rd October 1568, some twelve weeks before his death. [36]

So died Myles Coverdale, full of years, on 20th January 1569. Brook tells us that he *continued preaching as long as he was able; and died a most happy and comfortable death.* [37] Coverdale's own words written in exile nearly 30 years before his death are worthy of note: *O dear brethren, let us consider how great our sins are, for the which the innocent Son of God dieth. Justly ought all the world to be dead unto us in Christ, and we unto the world. He that learneth not to die in this life, is afraid when the hour of death cometh.... Death unto those that faithfully believe, is through the death of Christ become the gate to life; for their comfort and strong hope is in the words of Jesus when he saith 'he that believeth on Me shall live though he were dead already'.* [38]

He was buried in the chancel of the church of St Bartholemew, a vast crowd of mourners attending his funeral, including the Dowager Duchess of Suffolk and the Earl of Bedford. The inscription on his tomb in the church was as follows:

In memory
Of the most reverend Father
Miles Coverdale
Who died, aged 80 years.
This tomb contains the mortal remains of Coverdale,
Who having finished his labours,
Now lies at rest,
He was once the most faithful
And worthy Bishop of Exeter
A man remarkable for the uprightness of his life.
He lived to exceed the age of 80 years,
Having several times been unjustly sent into banishment;
And after being tossed about, and
Exposed to the various hardships of life,
The earth kindly received him into her bosom.

In 1840 St Bartholemew's Church was pulled down to make room for the Royal Exchange, and Coverdale's remains were moved to St Magnus Church, London Bridge, where they lie to this day in a tomb under the floor at the front of

Memorial tablet to Coverdale in St Magnus Church, London

the building. Over his tomb, is a panel of white marble, on a black slab, with a representation of an open Bible above it. The inscription is greatly worn, but reads:

To the memory of Miles Coverdale, who, convinced that the pure Word of God ought to be the sole rule of our faith and guide of our practice, laboured earnestly for its diffusion; and with the view of affording the means of reading and hearing in their own tongue the wonderful works of God not only to his own country, but to the nations that sit in darkness, and to every creature where so ever the English language might be spoken, he spent many years of his life in preparing a translation of the Scriptures. On the 4th of October, 1535, the first complete printed English version of The Bible was published under his direction. The parishioners of St. Magnus the Martyr, desirous of acknowledging the mercy of God, and calling to mind that Miles Coverdale was once rector of their parish, erected this monument to his memory, A.D. 1837.

How beautiful are the feet of them that preach the gospel of peace, and bring glad tidings of good things. Isaiah lii. 7.

Chapter 12

An Evaluation

Of a truth against thy holy child Jesus, whom thou hast anointed, both Herod and Pontius Pilate with the heathen and people of Israel, have gathered themselves together, to do whatsoever thy hand and thy council determined before to be done. And now Lord, behold their threatenings, and grant unto thy servants with all steadfast boldness to speak thy word: and stretch out thine hand, that healing and tokens and wonders may be done by the name of thy holy child Jesus. (Acts 4 block C)

In his authoritative 'History of the Reformation in England' D'Aubigne states that the Reformation could have been caused by the King, the Church or the Bible. He rejected the first two most emphatically as anything more than secondary catalysts. Henry VIII was fiercely independent, resentful of the way the Church refused him a divorce and willing to separate the state Church from Rome on that account. However he was no real friend of the Reformation, and the persecutions of 1509-32 and from 1539-47 in England of those who sincerely embraced the Reformation is testimony to his lack of any real affection to its principles. The Church was correct in identifying the Reformation as contrary to its teaching, especially on the all-important matter of what saves souls. Consequently, it consistently branded all true Reformers such as Coverdale as heretics.

The third force was the Bible and the religious and spiritual principles which it taught. The Cambridge scholars in 1521-

25 had chiefly the Greek New Testament of Erasmus, the Latin Vulgate of Jerome and Luther's writings. Some of the hand-copied English Lollard Scriptures were also available.

This was the small seed which over the first forty years of the Reformation in England became a sturdy sapling and saw a complete change in the direction of religious life. While progress at times was slow, and sometimes seemed to reverse, by the year of Coverdale's death Reformed Christianity reflected the beliefs and convictions of an increasing number of people in England, with resulting changes in society, politics, education and commerce. In this time the Middle Ages were left behind, and modern Britain was born.

This becomes more evident when one examines the next eighty years of English life, increasingly dominated (more particularly after 1588 and the defeat of the Spanish Armada), by the conflict between two Protestant parties, neither of which existed before the Reformation. They were the Anglicans with the monarch at their head, and the Puritans, increasingly unwilling to accept the Church of England settlement. This conflict came to a head in the civil wars of the 1640's.

Coverdale played a not insignificant part in the Reformation in England. It is by reading and understanding the spiritual and religious principles which moved him and others, and by observing the devotion and steadfast conviction of this little band of ministers and people, one arrives at an appreciation of what the Reformation was, what it achieved and how it spread.

Coverdale is best known for his Bible translation work. On the title page of the King James Version of the Bible the following statement is found to this day: *The Holy Bible containing the Old and New Testaments translated out of the original tongues and with the former translations diligently compared and revised by His Majesty's special command.* It is a mark of Coverdale's stature that he had a direct input into three of the four important *former translations* and an indirect influence on the fourth. This work was far more effectual in moving forward the Reformation than Henry VIII's assuming the place of the Pope as Head of the Church of England, or Edward VI's Prayer Books, and took place in the teeth of the opposition of the Church of Rome.

Daniell estimates that from 1525 to 1640, some two million Bibles and parts of the Bible were printed in English for a population of around six million. He states: *To write about English life between 1525 and 1640 and take no account at all of such enormous popular demand as these totals demonstrate is surely to be perverse. Yet it is not only commonly done, it is the norm.* [1]

By 1543, when King Henry VIII's Act for the Advancement of True Religion outlawed the reading of the Bible, it becomes clear from the text of the Act how widespread Bible-reading had become. Among those to whom it was banned were *women, artificers, apprentices, journeymen, servingmen, husbandmen and labourers*. In the pages of Foxe, in the reigns of both Henry VIII and Mary, we frequently read of 'offenders' with little education, quoting Scripture to their accusers on contested points of doctrine. The Act exempted noblemen, gentlemen, substantial merchants and gentlewomen indicating that: *At the moment of his greatest power Henry VIII dared not wrest the Bible from the hands of the political classes.* [2]

The readership of the printed word, prompted by the availability of the Bible in English, began to increase. First one in a group, a village or a ward would read the chained Church Bible to others. Gradually literacy spread as more of the ordinary people were provoked into gaining this valued skill. It is widely recognised among linguists that the early Bibles had a profound influence on the English language.

Front page to New Testament: The Great Bible

Secondly, Coverdale was a noted preacher. He believed his calling was to teach others as opportunity presented: 'How shall they believe on Him of whom they have not heard? How shall they hear without a preacher? But how shall they hear except they be sent? As it is writ, *how beautiful are the feet of them that preach peace and bring good tidings.* (Romans 10 block C). In the reigns of Henry VIII, Edward VI and Elizabeth I he was called on at significant times to give the sermon at Paul's Cross, the most important preaching station in the country. Preaching was a part of his calling, and whether to small congregations or large, in London, Exeter, in exile or elsewhere, whether in English or German, he was for over forty years engaged in this important calling.

A third and rarely noticed activity complemented his other work: the translation of metrical psalms and hymns. The use of metrical psalms and hymns, as Coverdale saw them in Germany, Denmark and later Switzerland, was to encourage the people to become participants in congregational worship. It also provided a clear contrast to the Latin dirges and choir pieces of the pre-Reformation Church of England, sung by a select few to a passive audience. Although congregational singing did not take root in England until Elizabeth I came to the throne, Coverdale's clear-sightedness encouraged the trend twenty-five years before it became the norm. (For the first 150 years, the Church of England followed the Swiss practice and sang only psalms).

A fourth feature was his willingness to go into exile in 1528,1540 and 1555, with the danger and hardship involved – on the last two occasions with a wife and family – rather than stay in England and compromise. From the time he embraced the Reformation, when he was in mid-life, Coverdale spent a total of twenty years in exile rather than fall in with Tudor royal demands or go quietly along with the spirit of the age. In 1540, for example, he was part of the circle around an increasingly unpredictable King Henry VIII. Once the Act of Six Articles came into force the choice was stark to the early Reformers. Either compromise as did Cranmer who quietly sent away his wife in hopes of using his office to do some good as circumstances permitted, or leave the country as did Coverdale. It meant embracing a life of poverty rather than affluence, and reproach rather than promotion and honour.

Fifth, while in exile Coverdale translated a number of works of Luther, Calvin and others which he felt had been profitable to him, as well as writing several works of his own. In 1546, in the list of books forbidden by the law enacted in England, Coverdale heads the list with the first twelve. Two were his 1535 Bible and the separate New Testament which grew out of it. The others were almost all translations of Lutheran or

Swiss books or reissues of English works such as Wycliffe's 'Wicket'. This is a measure of Coverdale's forwardness in finding and sharing what he felt would be helpful to his countrymen in the works of Europe's leading Reformers.

Sixth, for a short time as Bishop of Exeter, Coverdale was in the forefront of the battle. In the midst of a people who had risen in rebellion against Edward VI, he was unwearied in his preaching and teaching, and in appointing and encouraging others where he felt they had a similar vocation. It was his conviction that this, rather than political activity or government legislation, was the ordained means to establish the Reformation in the hearts and lives of the people. He threw himself into this preaching in the certain knowledge that much was to be done and time was short. His example strengthened and energised the work of Reformation in those parts.

Seventh, Coverdale was prepared and fully expected to die for his beliefs. Once Queen Mary came to the throne, those who led the Reformation were faced with a choice: recant or burn. Mary and her advisers were persuaded that once the threat of a painful and certain death became a reality, most would recant. Her first victim, the Duke of Northumberland, architect of the nine-day reign of Lady Jane Grey, did so, becoming a Roman Catholic in his last week on earth in a vain attempt to save his skin. However, most of those who had embraced the Reformed religion stood firm, encouraging each other to constancy and firmness in the face of death. Had they not done so, the Reformation would have faltered. It could with equal truth be said of them, as wrote John Knox of Scotland's first martyr: *If ye will burn them, let them be burned in underground cellars; for the reek of Master Patrick Hamilton has infected as many as it blew upon.* [3] Coverdale was the only one who was honourably released without wavering. No other of the prominent Reformers was spared (some died in prison), except a few who escaped out of prison and out of the country through the slackness of their jailors, and a handful who recanted or conformed.

Eighth, Coverdale's time in Geneva during his third exile, and the influence of Calvin, brought him to full sympathy with the simplicity of worship and church discipline as practised in that city. John Knox, a member with him of the same church, took the Geneva Service Book back to Scotland as the basis from which to organise the Church of Scotland at the 1560 Reformation. In England, the best attempts of Grindal and the other returning exiles could not further move the 'halfly' reformed Church of England. It is noteworthy that Coverdale, who had helped with the early reforms and who had been a leader in the Church of England only a few short years before, could by 1560 no longer in conscience accept this position. His third exile persuaded him that more should be done in England, but the Church of England remained as at the end of Edward VI's reign, with little further change.

It was not until the crisis of 1565-6 that the bud of Puritanism began to appear in London among those dispossessed of their livings. In his old age Coverdale chose to encourage and be numbered with the Puritans rather than fall back into a quiet conformity to the Church of which he had been both a preacher and bishop.

Some have challenged the idea that Coverdale was a Puritan, especially because he accepted a living in the Church of England from 1564-6. However, the accumulated evidence pieced together leaves little doubt:

- His refusal of his bishopric which had been held open for him until his return
- His refusal to wear the vestments, for example on big occasions such as the ordination of Parker. It is not credible he would have worn them about his ordinary duties.

- His letter of protest, jointly with nineteen other ministers, at the deposition of ministers in 1565.

- The letter to the Swiss divines making clear that Coverdale would resign his living rather than conform

- His resignation of his parish ministry a few weeks after this letter was written

- His frequent preaching at The Minories where the Puritan movement began, and his association with the Duchess of Suffolk who was patron of that church.

The Willoughby tomb in Spilsby Church, Lincolnshire, where the Duchess of Suffolk and her second husband Richard Bertie are buried. A good friend to Coverdale she shared the hardships of the Marian exile and did much to support the Reformation preachers.

- He was one of the few preachers the separatists were willing to hear

- The testimony of his Puritan brethren, written a few years later, reflecting on this time: *And it may here also be noted that the most ancientest Fathers of this our country, as Master Coverdale ... could never be brought to yield or consent unto such things as are now forced with so great extremity.* [4]

Finally, Coverdale's marriage is noteworthy. Although fifty years of age when he married, Coverdale chose the same course as other ex-friars such as Martin Luther and fellow-translator John Rogers. Once he had forsaken the monastery, he clearly felt his vows of chastity were not lawful or Scriptural, and so he was free to marry. The references we have to his first wife suggest she was a loyal help-meet to him during the twenty-six years they lived together, though through many dangers.

The foregoing evaluation is not to suggest that Coverdale's career and judgement were without blemish. The testimony of John Bale was that he was of a gentle, yielding disposition. Coverdale was a peace-maker. This saved him, no doubt, from unnecessary contentions and strife, although he could be firm and decided when he felt a stand was needed. His defence of Barnes from the attacks of Dr John Standish was steely, as was his determination to die rather than recant in the reign of Mary. However, in general he comes across as modest, self-effacing and peaceable. He was content, for example, to see his great translation labours as work in progress, only of use until replaced by better. Sometimes, perhaps he should have spoken and written his convictions earlier than he did. For example, it would seem that Coverdale, at an early stage, was convinced that the Swiss were right and the Lutherans wrong on the issue of the Lord's Supper being entirely a spiritual service of remembrance. However, he was slow to put his views into print until Cranmer and Ridley, the leaders of the English Church, were ready to move forward, at which point he published the works of Wycliffe and Calvin on the subject.

At times, Coverdale's willingness to please drove him to decisions of a more compromising nature. Three examples stand out. First, it is difficult to understand his decision, being fully persuaded in his mind that repentance was a

Scriptural term and penance a product of false teaching, to use the two terms interchangeably in the 1535 Bible. That he was not entirely easy about this decision, is suggested by his felt need to explain in the preface that he did not mean penance in the traditional use of the term.

Secondly, he along with Cranmer and Ridley acted as judges in the burning of George van Parris during the reign of Edward VI. If Coverdale felt it was wrong, there is no protest on record. No doubt he was affected by the spirit of the age, but others such as John Foxe and Edward VI were not. The spirit of the age gave church leaders and magistrates power not just to keep order and punish wrongdoers, but also over the conscience and beliefs of men. This spirit had the weight of the Medieval Church of Rome behind it, but even Calvin's Geneva was infected. It took the Puritans and then the Nonconformists in England until 1689 and the Act of Toleration to subdue this spirit.

Thirdly, he was willing to wear the vestments as Bishop of Exeter, rather than reinforce the protest of his friends John Hooper and John Lasco. Had Coverdale supported Hooper in a united front in 1550-51, it is possible that they would have been quietly dropped from the Church of England ceremonies, thus removing a future bone of contention. It must also be noted that for the remainder of his life after his 1553 deprivation, his letters are signed *Myles Coverdale Quond. Exon*, suggesting he took some satisfaction from having been a bishop. However, despite these failings we have a life devoted to the cause of the Reformation.

Coverdale's life is an undoubted contrast: 38 years a loyal son of the Roman Catholic Church but then, a most decided change having taken place, a leading English Reformer. The preface he wrote to *The Old Faith* summarizes both that change which occurred in his own life and the difference it subsequently made in his conduct. First, the change of heart is described at the start of the preface:

Like as the almighty eternal God, three persons and one in substance, of his tender mercy and love, not only created man at the beginning after his own similitude and likeness, but also, when he was lost, most graciously redeemed him and brought him out of bondage... sendeth the message of his word unto him, sheweth him what case he is in, openeth his prison door.... We cannot deny but we have heard his holy message... And some (thanks be unto Him therefore) hath he brought out of darkness into His wonderful light, and out of the devil's service into the kingdom of his dear Son.

Coverdale went on to describe the change it made in life and practice, both of himself and the other Reformers. It is an apt reflection of the work of the second half of his life.

Wherefore let us, that have received the old true faith of Christ, not only be content to abide any storm of trouble for it; yea to be mocked, scorned, persecuted and put to death therefore, if it so please God but also unfeignedly, every man to his power, in his heart by fervent prayer, in his mouth by good words, and in all his body by virtuous conversation and good Christian works, help and labour, that the blessed word of God may have the due honour belonging thereto; ....that God may have of us better servants, our prince truer subjects, and our neighbours more unfeigned lovers ('love your neighbours, do good to them that hate you...') than many have been before us, Amen. [5]

Appendix One: Comparison of Bible versions

Psalm 23 – The four most important early English versions compared. This is an example of the refinements made in translation work between Coverdale's 1535 Bible and the 1611 King James Version

Coverdale 1535	The Great Bible 1539 and Book of Common Prayer	1560 Geneva Bible	1611 King James Version
1 The Lord is my shepherd, I can want nothing.	The Lord is my shepherd: therefore can I lack nothing	The Lord is my shepherd, I shall not want.	The Lord is my shepherd; I shall not want.
2 He feedeth me in a green pasture, and leadeth me to a fresh water.	He shall feed me in a green pasture: and lead me forth beside the waters of comfort.	He maketh me to rest in green pasture, and leadeth me by the still waters	He maketh me to lie down in green pastures: he leadeth me beside the still waters
3 He quickeneth my soul, and bringeth me forth in the way of righteousness for his name's sake.	He shall convert my soul: and bring me forth in the paths of righteousness, for his Name's sake	He restoreth my soul, and leadeth me in the paths of righteousness for his Name's sake	He restoreth my soul, and leadeth me in the paths of righteousness for his Name's sake
4 Though I should walk now in the valley of the shadow of death, yet I fear no evil, for thou art with me: thy staff and thy sheephook comfort me.	Yea, though I walk through the valley of the shadow of death, I will fear no evil: for thou art with me; thy rod and staff comfort me.	Yea, though I should walk through the valley of the shadow of death, I will fear no evil; for thou art with me: thy rod and staff they comfort me.	Yea, though I walk through the valley of the shadow of death, I will fear no evil; for thou art with me; thy rod and thy staff they comfort me.

5 Thou preparest a table before me against mine enemies: thou anointest my head with oil, and fillest my cup full.	Thou shalt prepare a table before me against them that trouble me: thou hast anointed my head with oil, and my cup shall be full.	Thou dost prepare a table before me in the sight of mine adversaries: thou dost anoint mine head with oil, and my cup runneth over.	Thou preparest a table before me in the presence of mine enemies: thou anointest my head with oil; my cup runneth over.
6 Oh let thy lovingkindness and mercy follow me all the days of my life, that I may dwell in the house of the Lord for ever.	But thy loving-kindness and mercy shall follow me all the days of my life: and I will dwell in the house of the Lord for ever.	Doubtless kindness and mercy shall follow me all the days of my life, and I shall remain a long season in the house of the Lord.	Surely goodness and mercy shall follow me all the days of my life: and I will dwell in the house of the Lord for ever.

Appendix Two: The Martyrdom of Joan Waste, an answer of Anne Askew

Two examples from over 280 burnt at the stake in the reign of Queen Mary and more than 30 in the reign of Henry VIII, carefully recorded by John Foxe. The New Testament mentioned in the first case may well have been Coverdale's, being so far as we can tell the cheapest and most widely available. (Acts and Monuments Vol 8 p249).

The 1st day of August 1556, suffered likewise in the town of Derby a certain poor godly honest woman, being blind from her birth, and unmarried, about the age of twenty-two, named Joan Waste…. And when she was about twelve or fourteen years old, she learned to knit hosen and sleeves and other things which in time she could do very well. In the time of Edward VI, of blessed memory, she gave herself daily to go to the church to hear divine service read in the vulgar tongue. And thus by hearing homilies and sermons, she became marvellously well affected to the religion then taught. So at length, having by her labour saved so much money as would buy her a New Testament, she caused one to be provided for her. And though she was herself unlearned, and by reason of her blindness unable to read, yet for the great desire she had to understand, and have printed in her memory the sayings of holy Scriptures, she acquainted herself chiefly with one John Hurt, then prisoner in the common hall of Derby for debts.

The same John being a sober grave man, and being a prisoner, and many times idle and without company, did for his exercise daily read unto her some one chapter of the New Testament…. By which exercise she so profited, that she was able not only to recite many chapters of the New Testament without book, but also could aptly impugn (reprove), by many places of Scriptures, as well sin, as such abuses in religion, as then were too much in use in many persons. As this godly woman thus daily increased in the knowledge of God's holy word, and no less in her life expressed the virtuous fruits and exercise of the same: not long after, through the fatal death of blessed King Edward, followed the woeful ruin of religion in the reign of queen Mary, his sister. In which alteration, notwithstanding the general backsliding of the greatest part and multitude of the whole realm into the old papism again, yet this poor blind woman continued in a constant conscience, both being zealous in that she had learned, and also refusing to communicate in religion with those who taught contrary doctrine.

(Foxe proceeds to give an account of her examination before the Bishop). *And the sermon thus ended, the blessed servant of God was carried away from the said church, to a place called the Windmill pit, and holding her brother by the hand she prepared herself and desired the people to pray for her, and cried upon Christ to have mercy upon her as long as life served.* (She was burned at the stake in August 1556. Foxe lists names of several living who could verify this account, knowing there were *plenty of people who condemn his writings as untruthful* p247-50 Vol 8 Acts and Monuments Foxe).

Part of the examination of Anne Askew, burnt at the stake in 1546 under the Act of Six Articles in the reign of Henry VIII for denying transubstantiation. *Then would they needs know, if I would deny the sacrament to be Christ's body and blood. I said 'yea', for the same Son of God that was born of the Virgin Mary, is now glorious in heaven, and will come again in the latter day as He went up. And as for what you call your God, it is a piece of bread. For a more proof thereof, let it but lie in the box three months, and it will be mouldy, and so turn to nothing that is good. Whereupon I am persuaded that it cannot be God. 'God is a Spirit, and will be worshipped in spirit and truth'.* (p546 Vol 5 Foxe).

Appendix Three: Coverdale's most important literary works

Title	Year of Production	Comments
Translations of Psalms and Song of Solomon/Ecclesiastes	1534-5	First attempts at translation work while in exile. Coverdale's motive was to share with English people what himself had found profitable.
First English Bible since printing began	1535	Printed while still in exile. Reprints: 1537 (x2), 1550, 1552
Concordance of New Testament	1535	For the better study of Scripture. Printed in London
Ghostly Psalms and Spiritual Songs drawn out of Holy Scripture	1536	The one surviving copy in Queen's College, Oxford library is set to simple music. This book of psalms and hymns was a first attempt to import an important element of the German Reformation into England
A very excellent and sweet exposition upon the 22nd Psalm	1537	A translation from German of Luther of Psalm 23 (Coverdale's 1535 Bible follows the Vulgate in the numbering of Psalms).
The New Testament both in Latin and English	1538	This parallel New Testament was designed to help priests, who perhaps knew some Latin, to obey the injunctions issued by Cromwell and Cranmer to read the Bible in English in the churches
Exposition of the Magnificat	1538	Translation of Luther's commentary on Mary's song from Luke 1.
Latin/English New Testament	1539	Published after Cromwell's injunction ordering every priest to possess a copy of the Latin-English Bible
The Great Bible	1539	Begun in Paris, finished in London. The second edition of 1540 has Cranmer's preface, and so the Great

		Bible is often inaccurately called Cranmer's Bible. The psalms are in the Book of Common Prayer 1548 and all further editions including 1662.
Fruitful lessons upon the Passion, Burial, Resurrection, Ascension and sending of the Holy Spirit	1540	This work was based on Zwingli, but greatly expanded by Coverdale. It contains Scripture readings followed by some brief thoughts on the readings. This is the first sign of Swiss influence on Coverdale and the first significant work from his second exile.
The Old Faith	1541	A translation from the work of the Swiss Divine Bullinger, designed to show that the Reformation was not a new movement, but a revival of primitive New Testament Christianity.
Confutation of the Treatise of John Standish	1541	An answer to one who wrote against Robert Barnes after his martyrdom.
Acts of the Disputation in the Council holden at Regensburg. Supplication to King Ferdinand in the cause of Christian religion	1542	These two works, translated from Bucer and Melancthon, informed English readers of the increasingly sharp dispute in Germany between Lutherans and Emperor.
The Order that the Church and Congregation of Christ in Denmark and many places of Germany doth use.	1544	Designed to whet the appetite for change in England where the Reformation had come to a standstill.
New edition of Wycliffe's Wicket, edited by Coverdale.	1548	Coverdale, in the preface to this work, states that it was as clear and Scriptural refutation of the Roman Catholic teaching on transubstantiation as any he

		had seen. This was to be a key point of dispute between Queen Mary's bishops and the martyrs 1553-8.
Erasmus Paraphrase of New Testament Vol 2	1549	This project was in hand before Coverdale's return from his second exile at the initiative of Queen Katherine Parr. He had the largest share in producing the second volume.
A Spiritual Pearl	1550	Translated from Zurich minister Werdmuller by request of Duke of Somerset to his great comfort during his first imprisonment.
Three further Werdmuller treatises.	1555	Translates three more of Werdmuller's treatises from German
Certain Godly fruitful and comfortable letters	1564	A collection of letters of the martyrs, many of which went into Foxe's Book of Martyrs second edition of 1570.

Coverdale's writings condemned and burnt in 1546 by order of the bishops. (Foxe Vol 5 p567)

The Whole Bible 1535

The New Testament.
 A General Confession,
The Acts of the Disputation in the council of the Empire at Regensburgh.
A Short Recapitulation or Abridgment,
A Confutation touching the Protestation of Dr. Barnes.
The Christian State of Matrimony.
 A very excellent and Sweet Exposition upon the xxii. Psalm of David, called in Latin, *Dominus regit me*.
The Old Faith.
The Order that the church and congregation of Christ in Denmark, and in many other places of Germany, doth use at the Supper of the Lord, and at the ministration of the blessed sacrament of Baptism and Holy Wedlock.
A Faithful and True Prognostication upon the year 1536, translated out of high Almain into English.
Psalms and Songs, drawn out of Holy Scripture

Appendix Four: Letter written by Coverdale in anticipation of being burned at the stake

Letter written by Coverdale in 1554 to an Exeter friend while he, along with most other Reformation preachers, were in prison expecting condemnation and burning. (Western manuscript collection, Emmanuel College Cambridge Mss 260, f 178). Judging by the salutation, the friend is likely to have been John Bodley. Their paths crossed frequently from 1549.

- Bodley helped finance the expedition which put down the 1549 Prayer Book rebellion
- He was a near neighbour of Coverdale's in Exeter
- Bodley left England in 1555, joining the exiles first at Wesel, then at Geneva as it was unsafe for him to remain in England
- The sixth of his twelve children, and the first son born after he came to know Coverdale well, was named Miles, no doubt out of respect to the Reformer.
- He it was who set up the printing press and financed the Geneva Bible. It is likely that Coverdale joined the exiles at Geneva at his invitation
- Back in Elizabethan London, Coverdale was given a lectureship in the parish where Bodley and other friends resided.

The gracious comfort of the Holy Ghost, with the worthy increase of those notable gifts which he himself hath placed in your right worshipful person, continue and remain with you for ever, Amen.

It much rejoiceth my poor heart, in the midst of all storms and tempests, when I consider that there be some godly minded men which would be loath that I, which have put my hand to the plough, should now look backward, or for the pleasures of some, which last but the twinkling of an eye, should now in my age give over my part in Christ, and refuse the inheritance which he so graciously hath promised unto those that in the confession of his name endure to the end.

And although I have just occasion to be sorry that so many synstrall suspicions, surmises, lies and untrue reports go abroad as well of me as of others, yet my comfort on the other side whereof I spake before, doth even devour and swallow up all such heaviness, and that the more because the mouth of Him that never lied doth pronounce and say, 'Blessed are ye when men shall revile you and persecute you, and falsely speak all manner of evil reports against you for my sake, rejoice and be glad, for great is your reward in heaven'.

And again it is no small comfort to me and us all to remember that when God suffered not sinners long to follow their own minds but shortly correcteth them, as the scripture saith, it is a true evidence of his great lovingkindness, for this grace have the children of God more than the people that they are not suffered to go on still unpunished like other nations but are corrected by God by adversity, and yet so that He never withdraweth His mercy from them nor forsaketh them.

It cannot be denied that though it hath pleased God of His infinite goodness to bless this realm with special knowledge to His holy word, now of late more than afore, when all things were wrapped in Latin letters, there hath yet appeared and been declared amongst us special unthankfulness of God's goodness, special vanity and wanton receiving of such His mercy and benefits.

We have indeed heard much, talked much and some have written much of God's most reverend truth, but alas, what one estate amongst us hath been fervently given to love it and of love, earnestly to follow it. Have not all sorts of men generally now at this last in like manner loathed it and forsaken the most wholesome counsels of it, which yet still from time to time hath called us to repentance.

O just and righteous is God, that therefore sendeth strong delusions. Truly most marvellous is His mercy that yet preserveth some from believing lies and from giving themselves over into lewd minds. And how worthily were we served, if we that would not when we might, should have nothing at our own desire, no truth, no light, no gospel, no right religion, no mind nor grace at all to do well, but all falsehood, all darkness, all lies, all idolatry, with such disposition of life and manners as is only wicked, ungodly, corrupt and nothing else.

The effect of which tale, as unworthy a messenger as I have been, I told your countrymen (in Devon) oft and many times as faithfully and as truely as I could. And God of His accustomed mercy, I doubt not, hath opened the hearts of some, although the forward and evil minded wax worse and worse and wilfully get them into Egypt to their vomit again, whereas I am assured their melons and cucumbers, their garlic, onions and leeks, and all the cheer they can make, as fast as they dance about the calf, can do them little good; so sour a sauce is mixed with their sweet meats, and so horrible a thing it is to fall into the hands of the living God.

And as for me, I have entered my account with the Lord my God, who of His mercy, I doubt not, will make it up and graciously perform his promise. I have cast my pennyworth already, as evil an auditor as I am, what this ware will cost me, being fully appointed never to consent to unlawful things for any pleasure of life. How horrible things are contained in the mass book I learned many years ago, which as I utterly abhor, and all other idolatry, superstition, witchcraft, filthiness, sodomitish chastity, pilgrimages and images, even so my conscience and I, upon the most sure ground of God's holy commandments, God's fatherly promises and most undoubted example and practice of his old holy and ancient children, are at a sure point and steadfast determination never to return into Egypt, never to kiss the calf, never to meddle with my old vomit, never to be defiled with strange meats, never to worship Nebuchadnezzar's golden image, never to receive the beast's mark, never to shake hands with the devil, never to take of him other wages or livery, and to be short, never to forsake, refuse or recant the word of life, or for a kiss of the whorish world to profess myself into Judas religion. Sure I am, though the flail of adversity beat never so hard, and the wind of affliction blow never so sore, it shall but break my straw and blow away my chaff, for the corn that the Lord hath appointed for His own barn shall be safe enough, and kept full well by the help of Him that is owner thereof, to whom be all honour and praise, who also lend us His Holy Spirit that we may taste and see how friendly He is and what things He hath done, doeth at this present, and yet offereth to do for our souls. Amen.

Notes to the Chapters

Quotations from the Acts and Monuments of John Foxe are from the 8-volume Pratt edition of 1870 issued by the RTS. Some but not all of Coverdale's writings are found in the two volume set issued by the Parker Society: Coverdale's Remains (1846) and Coverdale's Works (1844).

Chapters 1 Introduction
- 1   p186   The English Reformation by A G Dickens Collins 1967
- 2   p236 Coverdale's Works: Fruitful Lessons upon the Passion of Christ

2 England before the Reformation
- 1   p 192 Memorials of the Martyrs C Taylor RTS
- 2   p4-5 The Age of Reformation by A Ryrie Routledge 2017
- 3   p 37 Acts and Monuments Foxe Vol 1 1870 RTS
- 4   p1 Coverdale and his Bibles. J F Mozley 1953 J Clarke
- 5   Folger Institute website
- 6   A Catalogue of the Bishops of Exeter J Hooker
- 7   P7-9 The Age of Reformation by A Ryrie Routledge 2017
- 8   p 10 The Music of the English Parish Church by Timperley
- 9   p18 The Peoples Bible: D Wilson Lion Hudson 2010
- 10   p10 The Age of Reformation by A Ryrie Routledge 2017
- 11   A Catalogue of the Bishops of Exeter
- 12   p37 Laferrierre, (Austin Friars in pre-Reformation England), Oxford University dissertation 2017
- 13   p 49 ibid
- 14   p 140 ibid
- 15   p 241 ibid
- 16   p 220 Roman Catholicism Lorraine Boettner BoT 1971
- 17   Acts of Parliament Henry IV 2.28
- 18   p 457 Vol 2 Laws and Canons of the Church of England Oxford 1851
- 19   p 86 Vol 1 Acts and Monuments Foxe
- 20   P381 Coverdale's Works. Fruitful Lessons

Chapter 3: The Dawn of the Reformation
- 1   p22 Vol 1 History of the Reformation in England D'Aubigne BoT (1962)
- 2   p30 Memorials of Coverdale S Bagster 1838
- 3   p5-6 Coverdale's Works Preface to the Old Faith
- 4   p393 Coverdale's Works Confutation of John Standish

5   p30   John Wycliffe by D Fountain   Mayflower Books 1971
6   p381   Reformation Studies by A G Dickens   Hambledon 1982
7   p32   The People's Bible by D Wilson   Lion 2011
8   p89   The Erasmus Reader
9   p18   Triumph of Truth   D'Aubigne   Bob Jones University Press 1996
10   p26   ibid
11   p153   Martin Luther Booth Barbour   EP 1988
12   p633   Vol 4 Acts and Monuments Foxe
13   p35   Archbishop Grindal by Colinson   Cape 1959
14   p3   Coverdale and His Bibles J F Mozley J Clarke 1953
15   p374   Coverdale's Works   Fruitful Lessons
16   p432   Coverdale's Remains   Confutation of John Standish
17   p13   Coverdale's Remains   Preface to 1535 Bible
18   p437   Vol 5   Acts and Monuments Foxe
19   p335   Latimer's Sermons   Parker ed.
20   p36   John Frith: Scholar and Martyr B Raynor   Pond View Books
21   p427   Vol 5   Acts and Monuments   Foxe
21a   p766 Vol 4 Acts and Monuments Foxe
22   p768   Vol 4   Acts and Monuments   Foxe
23   mss 270 f 178   Emmanuel College, Cambridge
24   p40 Vol 5   Acts and Monuments Foxe
25   p41   Vol 5   Acts and Monuments Foxe
26   p490   Coverdale's Remains   Letters
27   State Papers of Henry VIII
28   p182   W Tyndale: A Biography   by D Daniell   Yale UP 1994
29   p6   Gleanings of the Common Place Book of John Hooker   ed Harte 1926
30   p130   Vol 5   Acts and Monuments   Foxe

Chapter 4: First Exile – The 1535 Coverdale Bible
    1   p153   The Bible in English   D Daniell Yale UP 2003
    2   Wegg – Antwerp (1477-1559) Published 1916
    3   London's Triumphant Merchant Adventurers and the Tudor City
    4   P6   Coverdale and his Bibles   J F Mozley Clarke 1953
    5   P591 Vol 6   The Acts and Monuments J Foxe
    6   P18   C Hine Reformation magazine May 2020
    7   P132 C S Lewis   Select Literary Essays 1951
    8   P109   J F Mozley   Coverdale and his Bibles
    9   P72   ibid
    10   P 537 Vol 2 The Gentleman's Magazine May 1835
    11   P39   Memorials of Coverdale S Bagster 1838

12 P120 Mozley citing letter by W Latimer from Bodleian Quarterly Review
13 P 53 Lansdowne 981, letter by W Fulke 1583. British Library
14 P 121 The Making of the English Bible Daniell Yale 2003
15 A F Wikgren The Coverdale Bible 1535 Book Club of California 1974

Chapter 5:   Working for Thomas Cromwell
1   p22 Vol 1   Macaulay The History of England   Everyman 1946
2   p773   Wilkins Concordia
3   English Monasteries on the Eve of Dissolution   by A Savine
4   p14   Queen Elizabeth I J E Neale 1952
5   Vol 10 Jan-July 1536   Letters and Papers of Henry VIII
6   p 151 Gospel Standard May 1856   J C Philpott
7   p537   Coverdale's Remains   Parker Society
8   p537   Coverdale's Remains
9   p25   Coverdale's Remains
10   p122 Vol 11   L Lupton History of the Geneva Bible   Olive Press 1979
11   p261   Coverdale and his Bibles J F Mozley
11a p191   The English Reformation by A G Dickens   Collins 1967
12   p492   Coverdale's Remains
13   p 411 Vol 5   The Acts and Monuments   J Foxe
14   p 211 Coverdale and his Bibles Mozley
14a p 64 Memorials of Cranmer by J Strype
15   p499   Coverdale's Remains
16   p 500 Coverdale's Remains
17   p501 Coverdale's Remains
18   Fasti Ecclesiae Anglicanae 1300-1541 Salisbury Diocese (pub 1962)
19   P 472 A Chapter in International Protestantism: Myles Coverdale Henrician Migrant (Harland Unpublished dissertation Yale 1967)

Chapter 6:   Second Exile; suffering reproach
1   p654 Vol 5 Acts and Monuments Foxe
2   p419   ibid
2a   p 25 Add. Ms 26670 British Library
3   p566   Vol 5 Acts and Monuments Foxe
3a   p482 Coverdale's Works
3b   p196 Zurich Letters 1549-53 volume (Parker)
3c   p502   Coverdale's Remains (Parker)
3d   p245 Zurich Letter 1549-53 volume.

4   p525 Coverdale's Remains (Parker)
5   p519 Luther on the Galatians (James Clarke 1972)
6   p 325 Coverdale's Remains
7   p313 ibid
8   p345 ibid
9   p 325 ibid
10 Preface to The Order of the Churches in Denmark p467 Works
11 P 175 Vol 11 A History of the Geneva Bible L Lupton (Olive Press) 1979
12 P29 Vol 1 Works of Thomas Becon (Parker Society)
12a p 497 Coverdale's Remains (Parker Society)
13 P274 Vol 1 Latimer's Sermons (Parker Society)
14 P 10 Vol 12 A History of the Geneva Bible L Lupton
15 P503 Coverdale's Remains
16 P 507 ibid
17 Cited p322 Coverdale and his Bibles J F Mozley
18 p 247 Zurich Letters (1549-53 volume) Parker Society

Chapter 7: The Reformation gathers pace
   1 p9 The British Josiah by Woychuk SMF Press 2001
   2 p35 ibid
   3 p365 Thomas Cranmer D MacCulloch Yale 1996
   4 p18 Timperley The Music of the English Parish Church Internet Archives.
   5 State Papers of Edward VI 1.55
   6 p 162 G Williams Wales and the Reformation Uiversity of Wales Press 1997
   7 Cited p410 Life of Thomas Cranmer by MacCulloch
   8 p 31 Vol 15 Works of John Owen Johnstone and Hunter 1861
   9 p 46 Vol 1 History of England Macaulay Dent 1946
   10 Cited in Martin Bucer by Greschat John Knox Press 2004
   11 MS Domestic Edward VI Vol 19
   12 p 232 Troubles at Frankfurt ed Arber 1908
   13 p 21 Common Place Book by John Hooker
   14 p 85 Vol 2 History of Exeter DCRO 1919
   15 p 182 The Western Rebellion, Rose-Troup Forgotten Books 2018
   16 p 201 ibid
   17 p 394 ibid
   18 MS Domestic Edward VI State Papers
   19 p 93 Coverdale's Works

Chapter 8: Bishop of Exeter
   1   p 272 Vol 1 Works of Latimer Parker Society
   2   p 488   Vol 2   Memorials by John Strype
   3   p 96 Common Place Book by John Hooker
   3a   Lansdowne 981 Ms British Library
   4   p18   p172 Rose-Troup The Western Rebellion of 1549
   5   p182 ibid
   6   p75 Siege of Exeter by Hooker
   7   Hooker's Catalogue of the Bishops of Exeter
   8   Lives of 22 English Divines S Clarke Underhill and Rothwell 1660
   9   Catalogue of the Bishops of Exeter by John Hooker
   10   ibid
   10a p110 Edward VI Chronicle (Internet Archive ed)
   10b The British Josiah by Wolchuk SMF Press 2001
   11   p 281 Vol 3 Works of John Knox BoT 2014
   12   p 414 Vol 5 Letters of Calvin BoT 2009
   13   p54 Vol 1 History of the Puritan by Daniel Neil Tegg 1837
   14   p 135 Age of Reformation by Ryrie Routledge 2017

Chapter 9: A Narrow Escape from Burning
   1   p11 Works of Nicholas Ridley Parker 1843
   2   p16 Gleanings of John Hooker
   3   p62 Works of Ridley
   3a p 328 PCA 1552-4
   4   p505   Vol 1 Zurich Letters from reigns of H8,E6,Mary
   5   Mss 270, f178 Emmanuel College, Cambridge
   6   p551-3 Vol 6 Foxe
   7   p722 Vol 6 Foxe Acts and Monuments
   8   p 157 Memorials of Myles Coverdale JJ Lowndes (1836)
   9   p 96   1554-6 PCA

Chapter 10: Third exile: A wanderer
   1   p260 VI University of Copenhagen a/c Danisk Magazine 1859
   2   p21 Coverdale and his Bibles Mozley
   3   p281 Troubles at Frankfurt ed Arbor 1908
   4   Foxe (I have not been able to relocate this quote in the limited time available)
   5   P160 Jan 1556 Zurich Letters
   6   P168 Aug 1557 ibid
   7   P527 Coverdale's Remains
   8   P363 The Marian Exiles by Garrett

9   P218   Troubles in Frankfurt
10 Mss 2523 ff 14-5 Papers of Richard Bertie
11 P 528   Coverdale's Remains
12 P 121 Vol XI 1897 RHS Trans
13 P 164 Zurich Letters
14 P 18 footnote The Marian Exiles Garrett
15 P 185   Troubles at Frankfurt
16 P 354   Official List
17 P 37-8 Autobiography of Sir Thomas Bodley   Bod Lib 2006
18 F 264
19 P 242 Martin
20 P3   Troubles at Frankfurt
21 P 228   ibid
22 P 71   Vol 1 Zurich Letters
23 P27 The Bible by Gordon Campbell   OUP 2010
24 P xliii Vol 1 Works of John Bunyan   BoT 1999
25 P 191 Vol 6 Calvin's Letters
26 P78 Vol 6 Works of John Knox
27 P 83-4 Vol 6   Works of John Knox
28 P 225   Troubles at Frankfurt

Chapter 11:   Return as an Early Puritan

1   p92   Queen Elizabeth I by J E Neale Cape 1937
2   p4 Vol 1   Strype's Annals of the Reformation
3   p101   ibid
4   p 219   ibid
5   p129   ibid
6   p61-2 Zurich Letters
7   p 59   The Elizabethan Puritan Movement Collinson (Cape)
8   p 7   ibid
8   p 258   Vol 1 Strype
9   p 10   Common Place Book of John Hooker
10 p 88 The Marian Exiles by M Garrett
11 p 23   Coverdale and his Bibles Mozley
11a p316   ibid
12 Photo by Mark C Grant at English Wikipedia
13 Clothworkers Court Book 11.57
14 Clothworkers Court Book 11.120
15 P 38 Vol VI   Acts and Monuments   Foxe
16 Introduction to Letters of the Martyrs by Coverdale
17 Coverdale and the making of Foxe's Book of Martyrs S Wabuda
18 Letter of Grindal to Cecil p 25   Mozley

223

19 P 136 Zurich Letters (Parker Society 1845)
20 Letter of Coverdale to Cecil p 25 Mozley
21 p 234 Wales and the Reformation Williams U of Wales 1997
22 p 31   Life of Bernard Gilpin by Wm Gilpin
23 p 127 Vol 1.2   Strype Annals of the Reformation
24 Mss 2000-19/2019   Lambeth Palace Library
25 p 139 Vol 6 Works of John Knox
26 p 121-4 Vol 2 Zurich Letters
27 p 137 ibid
28 p 148 Vol 1   History of the Puritans D Neal
29 p 227 John Knox and the Church of England by Lorimer H King 1875.
30 p153   Vol 1 History of the Puritans D Neal
31 p 170   Archbishop Grindal by Collinson Cape 1979
32 Coverdale's Letters 29th Jan 1564 (Parker)
33 p 120 House of the Minories by Ed Tomlinson
34 p 86   Elizabethan Puritan Movement Collinson
35 Harl 5827 leaf 46   Memorials of John Hooker
36 P 65   Elizabethan Nonconformity   Journal of Ecclesiastical History   17 (Apr 1966)
37 p 127 Vol 1   D Neal History of the Puritans
38 p 309   Coverdale's Works

Chapter 12:   An Evaluation
1 p 121 The Bible in English D Daniell Yale 2003
2 p 266 The Reformation in England   A G Dickens
3 p 11   History of the Reformation in Scotland J Knox   Melrose 1905
4 p 254 Troubles in Frankfurt   ed Arber 1908
5 p 1-5 being the Preface to The old Faith' Coverdale's Works

Index

Aarau 8, 159-160, 169
Advancement of True Religion, 1546 Act for 90, 197
Antwerp 46-50, 57, 71, 92, 121, 148
Armada 129, 196
Arundel Constitution, 17
Augsburg Interim 109, 154
Augsburg, Peace of 143, 155
Augustine of Hippo, 34-5, 61
Austin Friars and Friary 1, 13-14, 28, 33, 39-40, 69, 97

Bacon, Lord Francis 172, 174
Bale, John, 9, 33, 203
Barnes, Robert 33, 37-9, 89-92, 97, 203
Basle 144, 155, 175
Bedford, Lord John Russell, 1st Earl, 7, 123-4
Bedford, Lord John Russell 2nd Earl 128, 192
Bergzabern 101-2, 105-8, 155
Berne 144, 155, 159
Bertie, Richard 157-8, 172, 190, 202
Berwick, Treaty of 173
Beza, Theodore 160-1, 187
Bible, 21-23,
Bible:
Coverdale (1535) 2, 50-61, 67, 73, 196
Geneva (1560) 4 ,25, 71, 162-5
Great (1539) 55-6, 72-8, 90-1, 116, 126, 148, 165, 198, 210
King James (1611) 25, 46, 54, 165, 196, 206
Matthews (1537) 51, 57, 71-2, 75

Vulgate, 24-5, 51, 73, 196, 210
Wycliffe (1382) 18, 24

Bilney, Thomas 2,4,32-6, 43
Bodley, John 123, 129, 153, 159, 162, 168, 180, 214
Boleyn, Anne 42, 65-7, 171
Bonner, Edmund 77, 90-1, 112, 144, 148, 174
Bradford, John 2, 137, 143, 177, 181
Brett, John 158
Bucer, Martin 93, 104-6, 118-9, 130, 157, 211, 221
Bullinger, Henri 21, 94-8, 108, 130, 144, 176, 187

Calais 7, 86, 109, 121, 172
Calvin, John 3, 95-7, 114, 119, 138, 155, 161, 167, 199
Cambridge, 1,2, 13, 22, 32-9, 65, 89, 97-8, 120, 183
Campensis, Johannes 49
Cardinal College, Oxford, 36-7
Caxton, William, 10, 26
Catherine of Aragon 31, 59, 63, 65, 141
Cecil, Sir William 131, 172, 178, 182, 187
Charles V, Emperor 4,5,30-1, 46, 63, 86, 102, 109, 147, 151
Christian III of Denmark 3, 99, 149-150
Clark, John 36-7
Clement VII, Pope(1523-34) 63
Common Prayer, Book of
Commons, House of 63-5
Coverdale, Myles:
    Birth 8-9

Education 9,12-14, 34-6
Conversion 33-4
Leaves friary 39-40
Translates first Bible 50-61
Works for Cromwell 68-83
Germany and Denmark 91-109
  Bishop of Exeter 126-139
  Escapes burning 140-151
  In exile again 151 - 158
  At Geneva 160 - 168
  Refuses bishopric 176
  St Magnus 182-6
  Death 192
Coverdale, Elizabeth (wife) 13, 67, 81, 152
Coverdale, Kathryn (second wife) 13, 191
Cox, Richard 174
Cranmer, Thomas 2,65-7,73, 78,82, 86-7, 112-4, 116-9, 135-7, 204
Cromwell, Thomas 2,4,13,39, 42, 62-5, 67-8, 72-89, 210

D'Aubigne, J H Merle 20,28, 69, 195
Denmark 98-101, 136, 149, 152-3, 199

Edinburgh, Treaty of 172
Elizabeth I 67, 171-2, 177, 184, 188, 199
English House, Antwerp 48-50
Edward III 22-3
Edward VI 2,4, 65, 74, 100, 111-20, 130, 138, 141, 174, 200-1, 204
Emden 143
Erasmus, Deciderius 4, 24-6, 32, 45, 113, 162, 196
Exeter 123-4, 129-30, 144, 153, 161, 177, 198

Fagius, Paul 118
Ferdinand, King of Hungary 158, 211
Fisher, Bishop John 26, 62-4, 67-8
Flodden battlefield 6
Foxe, John 7,18, 41, 50, 77, 89, 113, 130, 148, 181-2, 197, 204, 209
Francis I, King of France 5, 77
Frankfurt 47, 93, 143, 158, 168, 187
Frederick, Elector of Saxony, 28, 30-1, 88, 109
Frith, John 32, 36-7, 43, 91
Fulke, William 52

Gardiner, Stephen, 38,77,82, 86-7,89-90, 110, 112, 144, 147
Geneva 3, 95, 129, 144, 161-2, 167-9, 178, 186, 190
Germany, Little, 33, 35
Gilby, Anthony 162
Goodman, Christopher 162
Grey, Lady Jane 115, 139-40, 153, 200
Grindal, Edmund, Bishop of London 143, 166, 175-6, 183, 187-89, 201
Guise, Mary, Scottish Queen Regent 188
Gutenberg Johannes 26

Hamburg 46-7, 57
Hele, Walter 134
Hampton Court Palace 16, 17
Henley 81
Herman, Richard 46, 47
Henry VIII 2-3, 9, 15, 23, 31, 43, 47, 58, 60, 62-3, 67, 71, 77, 84, 109-11, 113-4, 121, 139, 171, 195, 198-199, 209

High Commission, Court of 174, 187
Hitton, Thomas 43
Hooker, John 10, 13, 44, 124, 128, 133, 177
Hooper, John 2, 117, 124, 128, 136, 144, 148, 150, 177, 204
Hubert, Conrad 101-8, 131

James IV of Scotland 7
John, King of England 18

Kethe, William 129

Latimer, Hugh 2, 4, 32, 34-7, 67, 73, 87, 100, 127, 144, 170, 177
Lasco, John 136, 204
Latre, Guido 56
Leicester, Earl of 182-3
Leo X, Pope (1513-21) 14, 29
Lever, Thomas 137, 153, 155, 159
Lewis CS 53
Llandaff 182
Lollards 18, 22-6, 39-41
Lords, House of 134, 136
Luther, Martin 2, 14, 24, 27-31, 33, 38, 43, 46, 51, 69, 86, 89, 96, 102, 109, 154, 203

Macalpine, John 81, 99, 148, 152
Marburg 47, 56
Mary, Queen of England 111, 138-9, 149-150, 156, 171, 188, 200, 208
Mary, Queen of Scots 139, 171
Mass 1, 14-6, 19, 32, 40, 60, 86-7, 96, 117, 120, 146, 170
Matilda, Queen 63

Melancthon, Philip 31, 35, 98, 211
Merchant Adventurers 9, 49-50
Minories, The Church of 178, 190, 202
More, Thomas 31, 43, 62, 67
Muhlberg 109
Myllar, Andrew 26

Newbury 80, 81, 84
Nicholson, James 57, 69, 73
Northumberland, John Dudley, Duke of 125, 134, 137, 139, 200
Norwich 10, 12, 116

Oxford 17, 36-7, 43, 118, 130, 132, 144, 210, 218

Papal Bulls 30
Parr, Katherine 2, 111, 115, 171, 212
Philip II of Spain 147, 156
Pilkington, James 174, 176
Pole, Cardinal Reginald 147
Pollard, John 134
Prayer Book 7, 116, 120, 122, 135, 138, 167, 175, 197
Prayer Book Rebellion 2, 120, 133, 214
Prestwood, Thomas 123
Printing 10, 24, 26-7, 43, 49, 56-7, 60, 75-8, 114, 125, 188, 214
Prowse, John 68

Regnault, Francois 77
Renaissance 4, 22, 25-6, 64
Restraint of Appeals, Act of 64
Ridley, Nicholas 2, 6, 117, 130, 136-7, 142-4, 177, 181, 204
Rogers, John 2, 50-1, 57, 71-2, 75, 117, 143, 148, 177, 203

Rome, Church of 14, 26, 29, 64-5, 67, 81, 171, 175, 195, 197, 204

Sampson, Thomas 162
Sandys, Edwin 175
Scotland 6,10, 24,26, 82, 112, 121, 125, 165, 167, 172-3, 186-88, 201, 224
Seymour, Jane 73-4, 85, 88
Six Articles, Act of 87,92, 109, 113, 122, 199, 209
Somerset, Edward Seymour, Duke of 112, 121, 125, 134, 136, 212
St Magnus Church 183-4, 187, 191, 193
St Michael Paternoster Royal, Church of 179
Standish, Sir John 97, 203, 211, 219
Stokesley,John, Bishop of London 41, 43
Steeple Bumstead 93
Strasburg 92-6, 98-9, 105-6, 118, 130, 144, 156, 158, 175, 191
Suffolk, Duchess of 153,156, 192, 202

Tetzel, Johann 29
Thomae, Nicholas 101,107-8
Topley, Thomas 40
Tubingen 98
Tunstall, Cuthbert, Bishop of London / Durham 24,26,43-5, 59, 113
Tyndale, William 2,4,32,37,39, 43-7, 50-4, 56-8, 71-3, 91,148

Uniformity, Acts of 116,175
Urban V (Pope 1362-70), 22

Van Emerson, Margaret 46
Van Meteren, Jacob 56-8
Van Parris, George 130, 204
Vaughan, Steven 47
Vesey, John 127-28, 131
Vilvoorde 50, 52

Weinheim 156-7
Wentworth, Lord 129
Werdmuller, Otto 153, 212
Wesel 143, 154-59, 161, 214
Weston, Robert 133,184
Whitehead, David 174
Whittingham, William 163
Windsor Castle 116,119
Winter, Admiral Sir William 172
Wittenberg 14, 28, 29
Wolfgang, Count of Zweibrucken,101, 156
Wolsey, Cardinal Thomas 9, 16, 26, 36-8, 42-3, 46-7, 62-3, 89
Worms 31, 43, 45,150
Wycliffe, John 17, 22-24, 40, 113, 200, 203

York 8, 9, 13, 16,85

Zwingli, Ulrich 51, 93, 96, 98, 105, 108, 154, 220